Books of the Bible

Psalms

Extra Large Print—20 point

Easier-to-read King James

King James Today™

Title   Books of the Bible Psalms
                                    Extra Large Print 20 point

Subtitle .... Easier-to-read King James
                                    King James Today™

Series .... 19 (20 point)
Type.. Trade Paperback (US), Large Print
AU Prepared for Publication.... Paula Nafziger, Chaplain
Subject Heading...................... Religion/Spirituality
ISBN-13 978-1948136860

987654321

All scripture is from an easier-to-read King James Version, King James Today™

Cover: "And he shall be like a tree planted by the rivers of water..." Psalm 1:3a

Inside: "As for man, his days are as grass: as a flower of the field, so he flourishes." Psalm 103:15

The Book of PSALMS aka The Book of Praises

N.T. Key: Direct speaking of Christ appear in *italics*. Quotation of Christ, God, The Holy Spirit, Their messengers, or the Old Testament, appear in *italic underlined*. The Bible in its entirety is the Word of God.

KING JAMES TODAY™

What makes this contemporary King James Version easier-to-read?

• Unnecessary word endings "est, eth, st, th, and ith" are dropped, **e.g.**, build<u>est</u> (build), build<u>eth</u> (builds),do<u>st</u> (do), lie<u>th</u> (lie), sa<u>ith</u> (says).

• Old English is replaced **e.g.**, art (are), hither (here), nigh (near), oft (often), thee (you), thine (your), thou (you), thy (your) thyself (yourself), unto (to), wast (were), ye (you).

• Old English spelling is updated **e.g.**, labour (labor), licence (license), musick (music), publick (public), shew (show), wilt (will).

• Ye, you, you-ward, your, yours, and yourselves, referring to more than one person, is noted by a superscript P (for plural) **e.g.**, you[P].

• Spelling consistency for proper nouns **e.g.**, Balac (Balak), Elias (Elijah), Esaias (Isaiah), Jonas (Jonah), Noe (Noah), Osee (Hosea), Sion (Zion).

Comparison of scripture:
King **J**ames **V**ersion versus **K**ing **J**ames **T**oday:

Blessed is the man that walketh not in the counsel of the ungodly, nor standeth in the way of sinners, nor sitteth in the seat of the scornful. Psalm 1:1 **KJV**

Blessed is the man that walks not in the counsel of the ungodly, nor stands in the way of sinners, nor sits in the seat of the scornful. Psalm 1:1 **KJT**

Books of the Bible—Psalms

Your word
is a lamp to my feet,
and a light to my path.
Psalm 119:105

Introduction to The Book of Psalms
Commentary by A. R. Fausset 1871
(partial/edited/enhanced)

The <u>Hebrew</u> title of the book of Psalms is *Tehilim*, meaning "praises" or "hymns." The <u>Greek</u> title in the Septuagint (a translation made two hundred years before Christ) is psalmoi, from which we get the word "Psalms." This corresponds to the Hebrew word *mizmoi*. A Psalm is *[an ode, or song, whose singing is accompanied by an instrument, particularly the harp; a sacred song or hymn; a song composed on a divine subject and in praise of God.]*

More than one hundred Psalms are prefixed with superscriptions, which give one or more (and in one case, Psalm 60, all) of these particulars: the direction to the musician, the name of the author or the instrument, the style of the music or of the poetry, the subject or occasion.

The book of Psalms is often called "The Psalms of David," as he is the only author mentioned in the New Testament (Luke 20:42) and his name appears in more titles than any other writer. Besides about one-half of the Psalms in which David's name appears, Psalms 2 and 95 are also ascribed to him (Acts 4:25). He was probably the author of many other Psalms which appear without a name. He used great efforts to beautify the worship of the sanctuary. Among the two hundred eighty-eight Levites he appointed for singing and performing instrumental music, we find mentioned the "sons of Korah" (1 Chronicles 9:19); including Heman (1 Chronicles 6:33-38); and also Asaph (1 Chronicles 6:39-44); and Ethan (1 Chronicles 15:19). God was doubtless pleased to endow these men with the inspiration of His Spirit. To Asaph are ascribed twelve Psalms; to the sons of Korah, eleven, including the eighty-eighth, which is also ascribed to Heman, that being the only instance in which the name of the "son" (or descendant) is mentioned; and to Ethan, one. Solomon's name appears before the seventy-second and hundred twenty-seventh; and that of Moses before the ninetieth.

The book of Psalms contains one hundred fifty independent compositions. The Jews divided it into five books corresponding to the Five Books of Moses (First, Psalms 1-42; Second, Psalms 43-72; Third, Psalms 73-89; Fourth, Psalms 90-106; and Fifth, Psalms 107-150.)

The Psalms have a form and character peculiar

to themselves; and with individual diversities of style and subject, they all assimilate to that form, and together constitute a consistent system of moral truth. They are all poetical, and of that peculiar parallelism which distinguished Hebrew poetry. They are all lyrical, or songs adapted to musical instruments, and all religious lyrics, or such as were designed to be used in sanctuary worship.

The distinguishing feature of the Psalms is their devotional manner of writing. The doctrines of theology and precepts of pure morality are impressed with the Psalms. God's nature, attributes, perfections, and works of creation, providence, and grace are unfolded. In the highest conceptions of the most exalted verse, God's glorious supremacy over the principalities of heaven, earth, and hell, and His holy, wise, and powerful control of all material and immaterial agencies are celebrated. The great covenant of grace rests on the fundamental promise of a Redeemer, and like God's exhaustless mercy, is set forth in regards to the teaching of new-birth by the Spirit, forgiveness of sins, repentance toward God, and faith toward Jesus Christ. Its glorious results are the salvation of men "from the ends of the earth" [Acts 13:47] which are proclaimed in believing, prophetic prayer and thankful praise. The history of the life and character of a Christian is edifying when truth is illustrated in experience (which is what God's Word and Spirit produce.) Within Psalms the experience of the truly godly is detailed under God's influence "in words which the Holy Ghost" taught [1 Corinthians 2:13]. The whole inner life of the godly man is laid open. Christians of all ages have in Psalms the temptations, conflicts, perplexities, doubts, fears, penitent moanings, and overwhelming griefs on the one hand, and the joy and hope of pardoning mercy, the victory over the seductions of false-hearted flatterers, and deliverance from the power of Satan on the other by which to compare their own spiritual practices.

The historical summaries of the Psalms are rich in instruction. God's choice of the patriarchs, the sufferings of the Israelites in Egypt, their exodus, temptations of God, rebellions and calamities in the wilderness, settlement in Canaan, backslidings and reformations, all furnish illustrations of God's care and authority of His people.

Books of the Bible—Psalms

The promises and prophecies in the Psalms exhibit the relations of the book to the Messiah and His kingdom. David was God's chosen servant to rule His people as the head at once of the State and the Church, the lineal ancestor "according to the flesh" [Acts 2:30, Romans 1:3], of His adorable Son and His type, and in His official relations both in suffering and in triumph. Generally, David's trials by the ungodly depicted the trials of Christ, and his final success the success of Christ's kingdom. Typically, David uses language describing his feelings, which only finds its full meaning in the feelings of Christ. As such it is quoted and applied in the New Testament. And further, in view of the great promise (2 Samuel 7:12-16) to him and his seed, to which such frequent reference is made in the Psalms, David was inspired to know that though his earthly kingdom should perish, his spiritual would endure forever in the power, beneficence, and glory of Christ's. In repeating and amplifying that promise, David speaks not only as "a type," but "being a prophet, and knowing that God had sworn with an oath to him, that of the fruit of his loins, according to the flesh, he would raise up Christ to sit on his throne," through David is "foretold the sufferings of Christ and the glory that should follow." Christ's incarnation *[the act of assuming flesh, or of taking a human body and the nature of man]*, humiliating sorrows, persecution, and cruel death are disclosed in the plaintive cries of a despairing sufferer; and His resurrection and ascension, His eternal priesthood, His royal dignity, His prophetical office, the purchase and bestowal of the gifts of the Spirit, the conversion of the nations, the establishment, increase, and perpetuity of the Church, the end of time, and the blessedness of the righteous who acknowledge, and the ruin of the wicked who reject this King in Zion, are predicted in the language of assured confidence and joy." Our Savior, with His disciples, sang one of these hymns (a Psalm) on the night on which He was betrayed [Mathew 26:30]; He took from one Psalm [Psalm 22] the words in which He uttered the dreadful sorrows of His soul [Matthew 27:46], and died with Psalm 31:5 on His lips [Luke 23:46].

Introduction to the Psalms

Commentary by Albert Barnes 1884
(partial/edited/enhanced)

The word Tehilliym is derived from the verb hâlal to praise, as in the word "Hallelujah, Praise Yehovah." Praise, more than anything else, is the characteristic of the book.

The Psalms are mostly lyrical poetry adapted to the harp or lyre; to be used in connection with instrumental music; to be "sung," not "read." Lyric poetry is, for the most part, an expression of deep feeling, and has its foundation in feeling or emotion. It is not so much the fruit of the understanding as of the heart; not so much the creation of the imagination as the utterance of deep personal emotion. It embraces in its design and nature all kinds of feeling, and may be joyous, pensive, desponding, triumphant, according to the feelings of the author, or to the occasion, for all these utterances may be sung, or may be set to music, the varying tones of music being adapted to express them all. In the Psalms, composed by a considerable variety of individuals on many different occasions, we have the varied feelings of trouble, anguish, fear, hope, joy, trust, thankfulness, devotion to God, penitence for sin, and the exultation of forgiveness - the heart moved, and finding vent for its feelings in words adapted to the melody of the lyre, or the musical tones of the voice.

The religious and moral psalms indicate the joy that may spring up in the soul of man in times of distress and sorrow; songs that show that there "is" joy in the darkness of this world; songs which illustrate the power and the value of religion; songs with which men cheer themselves and each other in their journey toward the grave; songs which even the guilty may pour forth from hearts softened into penitence, and filled with thankfulness in the assurance of pardon.

Superscriptions

The beginning of Psalm 3 introduces a "superscription." Superscription is defined as: *[that which is written or engraved on the outside or above something else.]* For example, U.S. coins include a superscription "In God We Trust."

Jewish people who do not read Hebrew commonly use "The Holy Scriptures" 1917 JPS (Jewish Publication Society) version of the Masoretic Hebrew manuscripts. It is an authoritative translation from the original Hebrew into English. Non-Jewish people

(Gentiles) and Jews who accept the Old and New Testament as the complete word of God, commonly use "The Holy Bible."

Verse numbers in "The Holy Scriptures" may differ from the verse numbers in "The Holy Bible" because the The Holy Scriptures list superscriptions as separate verses. Most translations of the The Holy Bible list the superscription as a title/heading before the remaining verses, or include them as part of the initial verse itself, and begin numbering the verses after the superscription.

Superscriptions are recorded in one hundred and sixteen of the one hundred and fifty Psalms. They name of the author or the instrument, provide musical style or notations, give direction to the musician, describe the subject, occasion or circumstances surrounding the composition and other descriptive information. The authority of superscriptions is disputed by some biblical scholars.

Psalm or Psalms?

Psalms refers to a collection of 150 individual writings, each known as a Psalm,
e.g. Psalm 1 from The Book of Psalms.

Hebrew Acrostics

An acrostic is *[an arrangement of words in a text or verse in which the first letter(s) of the lines, taken in order, form the name of a person, the subject of a composition, a title, motto, word, phrase, pattern, or an alphabetical arrangement.]* It is believed the use of acrostics assisted with mneomic *[assisting the memory.]* Poems which consist of detached thoughts on a subject might include an acrostic.

# of verses each Hebrew consonant covers in "acrostic Psalms:"

Psalm	9-10	25	34	37
	2	1	1	2
Psalm	111	112	119	145
	1/2	1/2	8	1

The Hebrew alphabet consists of 22 letters— all of them consonants—all capitals, no punctuation. Hebrew reads RIGHT to left.
Example:
ALL LETTERS 22 OF CONSISTS ALPHABET HEBREW THE PUNCTUATION NO CAPITALS ALL CONSONANTS THEM OF LEFT TO RIGHT READS HEBREW

Approximate Modern Israeli pronunciation:

HEH	DAH-leht	GEE-mehl	BEHT	AH-lehf
ה 5	ד 4	ג 3	ב 2	א 1
He	Dalet	Gimel	Bet	Alef

YOOD	THET	KHEHT	ZAH-yeen	VAHV
י 10	ט 9	ח 8	ז 7	ו 6
Yod	Tet	Het	Zayin	Vav

SAH-mehkh	NOON	MEHM	LAH-mehd	KHAHF
ס 15	נ 14	מ 13	ל 12	כ 11
Samekh	Nun	Mem	Lamed	Kaf

REHSH	KOOF	TSAH-dee	PEH	AH-yeen
ר 20	ק 19	צ 18	פ 17	ע 16
Resh	Qof	Tsadi	Pe	Ayin

TAHV	SHEEN
ת 22	ש 21
Tav	Shin

Hebrew Alphabet

LORD

Many times in the Old Testament you'll notice the word **LORD** in capital letters. It is the Hebrew word Yehovah transliterated from Hebrew to English. The name of God/Yehovah in Hebrew is written as **YHVH**. Vowels were not recorded in written Hebrew, but were used when speaking orally. Biblical scholars do not know how the word YHVH is pronounced without vowels present.

Possible pronounciations are: Yahveh/Yahweh (YAH-way), Yehowah (YEH-o-wah), Yahuweh (YAH-u-weh), Yahawah (YAH-a-wah), and Yehovah (Yeh-o-vah.) Notice the confusion as to it being pronounced with two or three syllables, the sound of V or W, and whether vowels should be borrowed from the Hebrew names for God: Adonai or Elohim.

Most biblical scholars and linguists do not believe "Jehovah" is the proper pronunciation of YHWH. There was no letter J, nor the modern sound of J in ancient Hebrew. The Hebrew word Yeshua, <u>when transliterated to Greek then to English</u> is Jesus.)

Strong's definition of: **LORD** H3068
'Yehovah (yeh-ho-vaw')

(the) Self-Existent or Eternal; Jewish national name of God.

From H1961; *[to exist, i.e. be or become, come to pass.]*

Applicable Webster's definition: **Lord**: A master; one possessing supreme power and authority; ruler; governor; the Supreme Being. **God**: The Supreme Being; the eternal and infinite spirit, the creator, and the sovereign of the universe. **Existent**: Being; having being, essence or existence. **Eternal**: Without beginning or end of existence or duration; everlasting; endless; immortal; perpetual; ceaseless; unchangeable; existing at all times
without change.

Selah

The Hebrew word Selah is hard to define since it's origin, root word, and derivation is uncertain. No one knows exactly what the word means. It appears seventy-one times the book of Psalms, once in 2 Kings, and three times in Habakkuk.

Since it is used many times in Psalms, it is likely a musical term. If it came from the Hebrew word "calah" it would mean: *[to hang; measure or weigh in the balances.]* If it came from the Hebrew word "celah" it would mean: *[suspension (of music), i.e. pause.]* Suspension further defined is: *[temporary cessation; interruption; intermission]* while "pause" means: *[a stop; a cessation or intermission of action, of speaking, singing, playing or the like; a temporary stop or rest.]* Some biblical scholars believe Selah is a combination of two Hebrew words: *[to praise]* and *[to lift up.]*

Assuming it is a musical term it was likely used to give direction to the instrumentalists and singers as they played and sang the Psalms. It could mean to pause, take a breath, sing "a cappella" *[without instrument accompianment]*, play instruments without vocals, lift your hands in worship, vocalize prayers, or similar ideas.

When you see this word in the Bible, take a moment to pause, weigh the meaning of what you've read or heard, lift your hands in worship, praise God, or do all at once.

PSALMS

Books of the Bible—Psalms

1:1 Blessed is the man that walks not in the counsel of the ungodly, nor stands in the way of sinners, nor sits in the seat of the scornful.

2 But his delight is in the law of the LORD; and in his law does he meditate day and night.

3 And he shall be like a tree planted by the rivers of water, that brings forth his fruit in his season; his leaf also shall not wither; and whatsoever he does shall prosper.

4 The ungodly are not so: but are like the chaff which the wind drives away.

5 Therefore the ungodly shall not stand in the judgment, nor sinners in the congregation of the righteous.

6 For the LORD knows the way of the righteous: but the way of the ungodly shall perish.

2:1 Why do the heathen rage, and the people imagine a vain thing?

2 The kings of the earth set themselves, and the rulers take counsel together, against the LORD, and against his anointed, saying,

3 Let us break their bands asunder, and cast away their cords from us.

4 He that sits in the heavens shall laugh: the Lord shall have them in derision.

5 Then shall he speak to them in his wrath,

and vex them in his sore displeasure.

6 *Yet have I set my king upon
my holy hill of Zion.*

7 I will declare the decree: the LORD
has said to me, *You are my Son;
this day have I begotten you*.

8 *Ask of me, and I shall give you the heathen
for your inheritance, and the uttermost
parts of the earth for your possession.*

9 *You shall break them with a rod of iron; you
shall dash them in pieces like a potter's vessel.*

10 Be wise now therefore, O you[P] kings:
be instructed, you[P] judges of the earth.

11 Serve the LORD with fear, and
rejoice with trembling.

12 Kiss the Son, lest he be angry, and
you[P] perish from the way, when his
wrath is kindled but a little. Blessed are
all they that put their trust in him.

[A Psalm of David, when he fled
from Absalom his son.]

3 :1 LORD, how are they increased that trouble
me! many are they that rise up against me.
2 Many there be which say of my soul,
There is no help for him in God. Selah.
3 But you, O LORD, are a shield for me;

my glory, and the lifter up of my head.

4 I cried to the LORD with my voice, and he heard me out of his holy hill. Selah.

5 I laid me down and slept; I awaked; for the LORD sustained me.

6 I will not be afraid of ten thousands of people, that have set themselves against me round about.

7 Arise, O LORD; save me, O my God: for you have smitten all my enemies upon the cheek bone; you have broken the teeth of the ungodly.

8 Salvation belongs to the LORD: your blessing is upon your people. Selah.

[To the chief Musician on Neginoth, A Psalm of David.]

4:1 Hear me when I call, O God of my righteousness: you have enlarged me when I was in distress; have mercy upon me, and hear my prayer.

2 O you[P] sons of men, how long will you[P] turn my glory into shame? how long will you[P] love vanity, and seek after leasing? Selah.

3 But know that the LORD has set apart him that is godly for himself: the LORD will hear when I call to him.

4 Stand in awe, and sin not: commune

with your^p own heart upon your^p
bed, and be still. Selah.

5 Offer the sacrifices of righteousness,
and put your^p trust in the LORD.

6 There be many that say, Who will
show us any good? LORD, lift you up the
light of your countenance upon us.

7 You have put gladness in my heart,
more than in the time that their
corn and their wine increased.

8 I will both lay me down in peace, and sleep:
for you, LORD, only make me dwell in safety.

[To the chief Musician upon
Nehiloth, A Psalm of David.]

5:1 Give ear to my words, O LORD,
consider my meditation.

2 Hearken to the voice of my cry, my King,
and my God: for to you will I pray.

3 My voice shall you hear in the morning,
O LORD; in the morning will I direct
my prayer to you, and will look up.

4 For you are not a God that has pleasure in
wickedness: neither shall evil dwell with you.

5 The foolish shall not stand in your
sight: you hate all workers of iniquity.

6 You shall destroy them that speak leasing: the

LORD will abhor the bloody and deceitful man.

7 But as for me, I will come into your house in the multitude of your mercy: and in your fear will I worship toward your holy temple.

8 Lead me, O LORD, in your righteousness because of my enemies; make your way straight before my face.

9 For there is no faithfulness in their mouth; their inward part is very wickedness; their throat is an open sepulchre; they flatter with their tongue.

10 Destroy you them, O God; let them fall by their own counsels; cast them out in the multitude of their transgressions; for they have rebelled against you.

11 But let all those that put their trust in you rejoice: let them ever shout for joy, because you defend them: let them also that love your name be joyful in you.

12 For you, LORD, will bless the righteous; with favor will you compass him as with a shield.

[To the chief Musician on Neginoth upon Sheminith, A Psalm of David.]

6:1 O LORD, rebuke me not in your anger, neither chasten me in your hot displeasure.

2 Have mercy upon me, O LORD; for I am weak:

O LORD, heal me; for my bones are vexed.

3 My soul is also sore vexed: but
you, O LORD, how long?

4 Return, O LORD, deliver my soul: oh
save me for your mercies' sake.

5 For in death there is no remembrance of
you: in the grave who shall give you thanks?

6 I am weary with my groaning; all
the night make I my bed to swim; I
water my couch with my tears.

7 My eye is consumed because of grief; it
waxes old because of all my enemies.

8 Depart from me, all you[P] workers
of iniquity; for the LORD has heard
the voice of my weeping.

9 The LORD has heard my supplication;
the LORD will receive my prayer.

10 Let all my enemies be ashamed
and sore vexed: let them return
and be ashamed suddenly.

[Shiggaion of David, which he sang to the LORD,
concerning the words of Cush the Benjamite.]

7:1 O LORD my God, in you do I put
my trust: save me from all them
that persecute me, and deliver me:

2 Lest he tear my soul like a lion, rending it

in pieces, while there is none to deliver.

3 O LORD my God, If I have done this; if there be iniquity in my hands;

4 If I have rewarded evil to him that was at peace with me; (yea, I have delivered him that without cause is my enemy:)

5 Let the enemy persecute my soul, and take it; yea, let him tread down my life upon the earth, and lay my honor in the dust. Selah.

6 Arise, O LORD, in your anger, lift up yourself because of the rage of my enemies: and awake for me to the judgment that you have commanded.

7 So shall the congregation of the people compass you about: for their sakes therefore return you on high.

8 The LORD shall judge the people: judge me, O LORD, according to my righteousness, and according to my integrity that is in me.

9 Oh let the wickedness of the wicked come to an end; but establish the just: for the righteous God tries the hearts and reins.

10 My defense is of God, which saves the upright in heart.

11 God judges the righteous, and God is angry with the wicked every day.

12 If he turn not, he will whet his sword; he has bent his bow, and made it ready.

13 He has also prepared for him the instruments of death; he ordains his arrows against the persecutors.

14 Behold, he travails with iniquity, and has conceived mischief, and brought forth falsehood.

15 He made a pit, and dug it, and is fallen into the ditch which he made.

16 His mischief shall return upon his own head, and his violent dealing shall come down upon his own pate.

17 I will praise the LORD according to his righteousness: and will sing praise to the name of the LORD most high.

[To the chief Musician upon Gittith, A Psalm of David.]

8:1 O LORD, our Lord, how excellent is your name in all the earth! who have set your glory above the heavens.

2 Out of the mouth of babes and sucklings have you ordained strength because of your enemies, that you might still the enemy and the avenger.

3 When I consider your heavens, the work of your fingers, the moon and the stars, which you have ordained;

4 What is man, that you are mindful of him? and the son of man, that you visit him?

5 For you have made him a little lower than the angels, and have crowned him with glory and honor.

6 You made him to have dominion over the works of your hands; you have put all things under his feet:

7 All sheep and oxen, yea, and the beasts of the field;

8 The fowl of the air, and the fish of the sea, and whatsoever passes through the paths of the seas.

9 O LORD our Lord, how excellent is your name in all the earth!

[To the chief Musician upon Muthlabben, A Psalm of David.]

9:1 I will praise you, O LORD, with my whole heart; I will show forth all your marvellous works.

2 I will be glad and rejoice in you: I will sing praise to your name, O you most High.

3 When my enemies are turned back, they shall fall and perish at your presence.

4 For you have maintained my right and my cause; you sat in the throne judging right.

5 You have rebuked the heathen, you have destroyed the wicked, you have put out their name for ever and ever.

6 O you enemy, destructions are come to a perpetual end: and you have destroyed cities; their memorial is perished with them.

7 But the LORD shall endure for ever: he has prepared his throne for judgment.

8 And he shall judge the world in righteousness, he shall minister judgment to the people in uprightness.

9 The LORD also will be a refuge for the oppressed, a refuge in times of trouble.

10 And they that know your name will put their trust in you: for you, LORD, have not forsaken them that seek you.

11 Sing praises to the LORD, which dwells in Zion: declare among the people his doings.

12 When he makes inquisition for blood, he remembers them: he forgets not the cry of the humble.

13 Have mercy upon me, O LORD; consider my trouble which I suffer of them that hate me, you that lift me up from the gates of death:

14 That I may show forth all your praise in the gates of the daughter of Zion: I will rejoice in your salvation.

15 The heathen are sunk down in the pit that they made: in the net which they hid is their own foot taken.

16 The LORD is known by the judgment which he executes: the wicked is snared in the work of his own hands. Higgaion. Selah.

17 The wicked shall be turned into hell, and all the nations that forget God.

18 For the needy shall not always be forgotten: the expectation of the poor shall not perish for ever.

19 Arise, O LORD; let not man prevail: let the heathen be judged in your sight.

20 Put them in fear, O LORD: that the nations may know themselves to be but men. Selah.

10 :1 Why stand you afar off, O LORD? why hide you yourself in times of trouble?

2 The wicked in his pride does persecute the poor: let them be taken in the devices that they have imagined.

3 For the wicked boasts of his heart's desire, and blesses the covetous, whom the LORD abhors.

4 The wicked, through the pride of his countenance, will not seek after God: God is not in all his thoughts.

5 His ways are always grievous; your judgments are far above out of his sight: as for all his enemies, he puffs at them.

6 He has said in his heart, I shall not be moved: for I shall never be in adversity.

7 His mouth is full of cursing and deceit and fraud: under his tongue is mischief and vanity.

8 He sits in the lurking places of the villages: in the secret places does he murder the innocent: his eyes are privily set against the poor.

9 He lies in wait secretly as a lion in his den: he lies in wait to catch the poor: he does catch the poor, when he draws him into his net.

10 He crouches, and humbles himself, that the poor may fall by his strong ones.

11 He has said in his heart, God has forgotten: he hides his face; he will never see it.

12 Arise, O LORD; O God, lift up your hand: forget not the humble.

13 Wherefore does the wicked contemn God? he has said in his heart, You will not require it.

14 You have seen it; for you behold mischief and spite, to requite it with your hand: the poor commits himself to you; you are the helper of the fatherless.

15 Break you the arm of the wicked and the evil

man: seek out his wickedness till you find none.

16 The LORD is King for ever and ever: the heathen are perished out of his land.

17 LORD, you have heard the desire of the humble: you will prepare their heart, you will cause your ear to hear:

18 To judge the fatherless and the oppressed, that the man of the earth may no more oppress.

[To the chief Musician, A Psalm of David.]

11:1 In the LORD put I my trust: how say you^P to my soul, Flee as a bird to your^P mountain?
2 For, lo, the wicked bend their bow, they make ready their arrow upon the string, that they may privily shoot at the upright in heart.

3 If the foundations be destroyed, what can the righteous do?

4 The LORD is in his holy temple, the LORD's throne is in heaven: his eyes behold, his eyelids try, the children of men.

5 The LORD tries the righteous: but the wicked and him that loves violence his soul hates.

6 Upon the wicked he shall rain snares, fire and brimstone, and a horrible tempest: this shall be the portion of their cup.

7 For the righteous LORD loves righteousness; his countenance does behold the upright.

PSALM 12–13

[To the chief Musician upon
Sheminith, A Psalm of David.]

12:1 Help, LORD; for the godly man ceases; for the faithful fail from among the children of men.

2 They speak vanity every one with his neighbor: with flattering lips and with a double heart do they speak.

3 The LORD shall cut off all flattering lips, and the tongue that speaks proud things:

4 Who have said, With our tongue will we prevail; our lips are our own: who is lord over us?

5 *For the oppression of the poor, for the sighing of the needy, now will I arise*, says the LORD; *I will set him in safety from him that puffs at him*.

6 The words of the LORD are pure words: as silver tried in a furnace of earth, purified seven times.

7 You shall keep them, O LORD, you shall preserve them from this generation for ever.

8 The wicked walk on every side, when the vilest men are exalted.

[To the chief Musician, A Psalm of David.]

13:1 How long will you forget me, O LORD? for ever? how long will you hide your face from me?

2 How long shall I take counsel in my soul, having sorrow in my heart daily? how long shall my enemy be exalted over me?

3 Consider and hear me, O LORD my God: lighten my eyes, lest I sleep the sleep of death;

4 Lest my enemy say, I have prevailed against him; and those that trouble me rejoice when I am moved.

5 But I have trusted in your mercy; my heart shall rejoice in your salvation.

6 I will sing to the LORD, because he has dealt bountifully with me.

[To the chief Musician, A Psalm of David.]

14 **:1** The fool has said in his heart, There is no God. They are corrupt, they have done abominable works, there is none that does good.

2 The LORD looked down from heaven upon the children of men, to see if there were any that did understand, and seek God.

3 They are all gone aside, they are all together become filthy: there is none that does good, no, not one.

4 Have all the workers of iniquity no knowledge? who eat up my people as they eat bread, and call not upon the LORD.

PSALM 14–15

5 There were they in great fear: for God is in the generation of the righteous.

6 You^P have shamed the counsel of the poor, because the LORD is his refuge.

7 Oh that the salvation of Israel were come out of Zion! when the LORD brings back the captivity of his people, Jacob shall rejoice, and Israel shall be glad.

[A Psalm of David.]

15:1 LORD, who shall abide in your tabernacle? who shall dwell in your holy hill?

2 He that walks uprightly, and works righteousness, and speaks the truth in his heart.

3 He that backbites not with his tongue, nor does evil to his neighbor, nor takes up a reproach against his neighbor.

4 In whose eyes a vile person is contemned; but he honors them that fear the LORD. He that swears to his own hurt, and changes not.

5 He that puts not out his money to usury, nor takes reward against the innocent. He that does these things shall never be moved.

[Michtam of David.]

16 :1 Preserve me, O God: for in you do I put my trust.

2 O my soul, you have said to the LORD, You are my Lord: my goodness extends not to you;

3 But to the saints that are in the earth, and to the excellent, in whom is all my delight.

4 Their sorrows shall be multiplied that hasten after another god: their drink offerings of blood will I not offer, nor take up their names into my lips.

5 The LORD is the portion of my inheritance and of my cup: you maintain my lot.

6 The lines are fallen to me in pleasant places; yea, I have a goodly heritage.

7 I will bless the LORD, who has given me counsel: my reins also instruct me in the night seasons.

8 I have set the LORD always before me: because he is at my right hand, I shall not be moved.

9 Therefore my heart is glad, and my glory rejoices: my flesh also shall rest in hope.

10 For you will not leave my soul in hell; neither will you suffer your Holy One to see corruption.

11 You will show me the path of life: in your

presence is fulness of joy; at your right hand there are pleasures for evermore.

[A Prayer of David.]

17:1 Hear the right, O LORD, attend to my cry, give ear to my prayer, that goes not out of feigned lips.

2 Let my sentence come forth from your presence; let your eyes behold the things that are equal.

3 You have proved my heart; you have visited me in the night; you have tried me, and shall find nothing; I am purposed that my mouth shall not transgress.

4 Concerning the works of men, by the word of your lips I have kept me from the paths of the destroyer.

5 Hold up my goings in your paths, that my footsteps slip not.

6 I have called upon you, for you will hear me, O God: incline your ear to me, and hear my speech.

7 Show your marvellous lovingkindness, O you that save by your right hand them which put their trust in you from those that rise up against them.

8 Keep me as the apple of the eye, hide

me under the shadow of your wings,

9 From the wicked that oppress me, from my deadly enemies, who compass me about.

10 They are enclosed in their own fat: with their mouth they speak proudly.

11 They have now compassed us in our steps: they have set their eyes bowing down to the earth;

12 Like as a lion that is greedy of his prey, and as it were a young lion lurking in secret places.

13 Arise, O LORD, disappoint him, cast him down: deliver my soul from the wicked, which is your sword:

14 From men which are your hand, O LORD, from men of the world, which have their portion in this life, and whose belly you fill with your hid treasure: they are full of children, and leave the rest of their substance to their babes.

15 As for me, I will behold your face in righteousness: I shall be satisfied, when I awake, with your likeness.

PSALM 18

[To the chief Musician, A Psalm of David, the servant of the LORD, who spoke to the LORD the words of this song in the day that the LORD delivered him from the hand of all his enemies, and from the hand of Saul: And he said,]

18 :1 I will love you, O LORD, my strength.
2 The LORD is my rock, and my fortress, and my deliverer; my God, my strength, in whom I will trust; my buckler, and the horn of my salvation, and my high tower.

3 I will call upon the LORD, who is worthy to be praised: so shall I be saved from my enemies.

4 The sorrows of death compassed me, and the floods of ungodly men made me afraid.

5 The sorrows of hell compassed me about: the snares of death prevented me.

6 In my distress I called upon the LORD, and cried to my God: he heard my voice out of his temple, and my cry came before him, even into his ears.

7 Then the earth shook and trembled; the foundations also of the hills moved and were shaken, because he was wroth.

8 There went up a smoke out of his nostrils, and fire out of his mouth devoured: coals were kindled by it.

9 He bowed the heavens also, and came

down: and darkness was under his feet.

10 And he rode upon a cherub, and did fly: yea, he did fly upon the wings of the wind.

11 He made darkness his secret place; his pavilion round about him were dark waters and thick clouds of the skies.

12 At the brightness that was before him his thick clouds passed, hail stones and coals of fire.

13 The LORD also thundered in the heavens, and the Highest gave his voice; hail stones and coals of fire.

14 Yea, he sent out his arrows, and scattered them; and he shot out lightnings, and discomfited them.

15 Then the channels of waters were seen, and the foundations of the world were discovered at your rebuke, O LORD, at the blast of the breath of your nostrils.

16 He sent from above, he took me, he drew me out of many waters.

17 He delivered me from my strong enemy, and from them which hated me: for they were too strong for me.

18 They prevented me in the day of my calamity: but the LORD was my stay.

19 He brought me forth also into a large place;

he delivered me, because he delighted in me.

20 The LORD rewarded me according to my righteousness; according to the cleanness of my hands has he recompensed me.

21 For I have kept the ways of the LORD, and have not wickedly departed from my God.

22 For all his judgments were before me, and I did not put away his statutes from me.

23 I was also upright before him, and I kept myself from my iniquity.

24 Therefore has the LORD recompensed me according to my righteousness, according to the cleanness of my hands in his eyesight.

25 With the merciful you will show yourself merciful; with an upright man you will show yourself upright;

26 With the pure you will show yourself pure; and with the froward you will show yourself froward.

27 For you will save the afflicted people; but will bring down high looks.

28 For you will light my candle: the LORD my God will enlighten my darkness.

29 For by you I have run through a troop; and by my God have I leaped over a wall.

30 As for God, his way is perfect: the

word of the LORD is tried: he is a
buckler to all those that trust in him.

31 For who is God save the LORD?
or who is a rock save our God?

32 It is God that girds me with strength,
and makes my way perfect.

33 He makes my feet like hinds' feet,
and sets me upon my high places.

34 He teaches my hands to war, so that
a bow of steel is broken by my arms.

35 You have also given me the shield of your
salvation: and your right hand has held me
up, and your gentleness has made me great.

36 You have enlarged my steps under
me, that my feet did not slip.

37 I have pursued my enemies, and
overtaken them: neither did I turn
again till they were consumed.

38 I have wounded them that they were not
able to rise: they are fallen under my feet.

39 For you have girded me with strength
to the battle: you have subdued under
me those that rose up against me.

40 You have also given me the
necks of my enemies; that I might
destroy them that hate me.

41 They cried, but there was none to save them: even to the LORD, but he answered them not.

42 Then did I beat them small as the dust before the wind: I did cast them out as the dirt in the streets.

43 You have delivered me from the strivings of the people; and you have made me the head of the heathen: a people whom I have not known shall serve me.

44 As soon as they hear of me, they shall obey me: the strangers shall submit themselves to me.

45 The strangers shall fade away, and be afraid out of their close places.

46 The LORD lives; and blessed be my rock; and let the God of my salvation be exalted.

47 It is God that avenges me, and subdues the people under me.

48 He delivers me from my enemies: yea, you lift me up above those that rise up against me: you have delivered me from the violent man.

49 Therefore will I give thanks to you, O LORD, among the heathen, and sing praises to your name.

50 Great deliverance gives he to his king; and shows mercy to his anointed, to David, and to his seed for evermore.

[To the chief Musician, A Psalm of David.]

19:1 The heavens declare the glory of God; and the firmament shows his handywork.

2 Day to day utters speech, and night to night shows knowledge.

3 There is no speech nor language, where their voice is not heard.

4 Their line is gone out through all the earth, and their words to the end of the world. In them has he set a tabernacle for the sun,

5 Which is as a bridegroom coming out of his chamber, and rejoices as a strong man to run a race.

6 His going forth is from the end of the heaven, and his circuit to the ends of it: and there is nothing hid from the heat thereof.

7 The law of the LORD is perfect, converting the soul: the testimony of the LORD is sure, making wise the simple.

8 The statutes of the LORD are right, rejoicing the heart: the commandment of the LORD is pure, enlightening the eyes.

9 The fear of the LORD is clean, enduring for ever: the judgments of the LORD are true and righteous altogether.

10 More to be desired are they than gold,

yea, than much fine gold: sweeter also than honey and the honeycomb.

11 Moreover by them is your servant warned: and in keeping of them there is great reward.

12 Who can understand his errors? cleanse you me from secret faults.

13 Keep back your servant also from presumptuous sins; let them not have dominion over me: then shall I be upright, and I shall be innocent from the great transgression.

14 Let the words of my mouth, and the meditation of my heart, be acceptable in your sight, O LORD, my strength, and my redeemer.

[To the chief Musician, A Psalm of David.]

20 :1 The LORD hear you in the day of trouble; the name of the God of Jacob defend you;

2 Send you help from the sanctuary, and strengthen you out of Zion;

3 Remember all your offerings, and accept your burnt sacrifice; Selah.

4 Grant you according to your own heart, and fulfil all your counsel.

5 We will rejoice in your salvation, and in the name of our God we will set up our banners: the LORD fulfil all your petitions.

6 Now know I that the LORD saves his anointed; he will hear him from his holy heaven with the saving strength of his right hand.

7 Some trust in chariots, and some in horses: but we will remember the name of the LORD our God.

8 They are brought down and fallen: but we are risen, and stand upright.

9 Save, LORD: let the king hear us when we call.

[To the chief Musician, A Psalm of David.]

21 **:1** The king shall joy in your strength, O LORD; and in your salvation how greatly shall he rejoice!

2 You have given him his heart's desire, and have not withheld the request of his lips. Selah.

3 For you prevent him with the blessings of goodness: you set a crown of pure gold on his head.

4 He asked life of you, and you gave it him, even length of days for ever and ever.

5 His glory is great in your salvation: honor and majesty have you laid upon him.

6 For you have made him most blessed for ever: you have made him exceeding glad with your countenance.

7 For the king trusts in the LORD,

and through the mercy of the most
High he shall not be moved.

8 Your hand shall find out all your enemies: your right hand shall find out those that hate you.

9 You shall make them as a fiery oven
in the time of your anger: the LORD
shall swallow them up in his wrath,
and the fire shall devour them.

10 Their fruit shall you destroy from the earth,
and their seed from among the children of men.

11 For they intended evil against you:
they imagined a mischievous device,
which they are not able to perform.

12 Therefore shall you make them turn their
back, when you shall make ready your arrows
upon your strings against the face of them.

13 Be you exalted, LORD, in your own strength:
so will we sing and praise your power.

[To the chief Musician upon Aijeleth
Shahar, A Psalm of David.]

22 :**1** My God, my God, why have you
forsaken me? why are you so far from
helping me, and from the words of my roaring?
2 O my God, I cry in the day time, but you hear
not; and in the night season, and am not silent.
3 But you are holy, O you that

inhabit the praises of Israel.

4 Our fathers trusted in you: they trusted, and you did deliver them.

5 They cried to you, and were delivered: they trusted in you, and were not confounded.

6 But I am a worm, and no man; a reproach of men, and despised of the people.

7 All they that see me laugh me to scorn: they shoot out the lip, they shake the head, saying,

8 He trusted on the LORD that he would deliver him: let him deliver him, seeing he delighted in him.

9 But you are he that took me out of the womb: you did make me hope when I was upon my mother's breasts.

10 I was cast upon you from the womb: you are my God from my mother's belly.

11 Be not far from me; for trouble is near; for there is none to help.

12 Many bulls have compassed me: strong bulls of Bashan have beset me round.

13 They gaped upon me with their mouths, as a ravening and a roaring lion.

14 I am poured out like water, and all my bones are out of joint: my heart is like wax; it is melted in the midst of my bowels.

PSALM 22

15 My strength is dried up like a potsherd; and my tongue cleaves to my jaws; and you have brought me into the dust of death.

16 For dogs have compassed me: the assembly of the wicked have enclosed me: they pierced my hands and my feet.

17 I may tell all my bones: they look and stare upon me.

18 They part my garments among them, and cast lots upon my vesture.

19 But be not you far from me, O LORD: O my strength, haste you to help me.

20 Deliver my soul from the sword; my darling from the power of the dog.

21 Save me from the lion's mouth: for you have heard me from the horns of the unicorns.

22 I will declare your name to my brethren: in the midst of the congregation will I praise you.

23 You[P] that fear the LORD, praise him; all you[P] the seed of Jacob, glorify him; and fear him, all you[P] the seed of Israel.

24 For he has not despised nor abhorred the affliction of the afflicted; neither has he hid his face from him; but when he cried to him, he heard.

25 My praise shall be of you in the

great congregation: I will pay my
vows before them that fear him.

26 The meek shall eat and be satisfied:
they shall praise the LORD that seek
him: your[p] heart shall live for ever.

27 All the ends of the world shall remember
and turn to the LORD: and all the kindreds
of the nations shall worship before you.

28 For the kingdom is the LORD's: and
he is the governor among the nations.

29 All they that be fat upon earth shall
eat and worship: all they that go down
to the dust shall bow before him: and
none can keep alive his own soul.

30 A seed shall serve him; it shall be
accounted to the Lord for a generation.

31 They shall come, and shall declare
his righteousness to a people that shall
be born, that he has done this.

[A Psalm of David.]

23 :1 The LORD is my shepherd;
I shall not want.

2 He makes me to lie down in green pastures:
he leads me beside the still waters.

3 He restores my soul: he leads me in the
paths of righteousness for his name's sake.

4 Yea, though I walk through the valley of the shadow of death, I will fear no evil: for you are with me; your rod and your staff they comfort me.

5 You prepare a table before me in the presence of my enemies: you anoint my head with oil; my cup runs over.

6 Surely goodness and mercy shall follow me all the days of my life: and I will dwell in the house of the LORD for ever.

[A Psalm of David.]

24:**1** The earth is the LORD's, and the fulness thereof; the world, and they that dwell therein.

2 For he has founded it upon the seas, and established it upon the floods.

3 Who shall ascend into the hill of the LORD? or who shall stand in his holy place?

4 He that has clean hands, and a pure heart; who has not lifted up his soul to vanity, nor sworn deceitfully.

5 He shall receive the blessing from the LORD, and righteousness from the God of his salvation.

6 This is the generation of them that seek him, that seek your face, O Jacob. Selah.

7 Lift up your^p heads, O you^p gates; and

be you[P] lift up, you[P] everlasting doors;
and the King of glory shall come in.

8 Who is this King of glory? The LORD strong
and mighty, the LORD mighty in battle.

9 Lift up your[P] heads, O you[P] gates; even
lift them up, you[P] everlasting doors;
and the King of glory shall come in.

10 Who is this King of glory? The LORD of
hosts, he is the King of glory. Selah.

[A Psalm of David.]

25:1 Unto you, O LORD, do I lift up my soul.
2 O my God, I trust in you: let me not be
ashamed, let not my enemies triumph over me.

3 Yea, let none that wait on you be
ashamed: let them be ashamed
which transgress without cause.

4 Show me your ways, O LORD;
teach me your paths.

5 Lead me in your truth, and teach me:
for you are the God of my salvation;
on you do I wait all the day.

6 Remember, O LORD, your tender
mercies and your lovingkindnesses;
for they have been ever of old.

7 Remember not the sins of my youth, nor my transgressions: according to your mercy remember you me for your goodness' sake, O LORD.

8 Good and upright is the LORD: therefore will he teach sinners in the way.

9 The meek will he guide in judgment: and the meek will he teach his way.

10 All the paths of the LORD are mercy and truth to such as keep his covenant and his testimonies.

11 For your name's sake, O LORD, pardon my iniquity; for it is great.

12 What man is he that fears the LORD? him shall he teach in the way that he shall choose.

13 His soul shall dwell at ease; and his seed shall inherit the earth.

14 The secret of the LORD is with them that fear him; and he will show them his covenant.

15 My eyes are ever toward the LORD; for he shall pluck my feet out of the net.

16 Turn you to me, and have mercy upon me; for I am desolate and afflicted.

17 The troubles of my heart are enlarged: O bring you me out of my distresses.

18 Look upon my affliction and my

pain; and forgive all my sins.

19 Consider my enemies; for they are many; and they hate me with cruel hatred.

20 O keep my soul, and deliver me: let me not be ashamed; for I put my trust in you.

21 Let integrity and uprightness preserve me; for I wait on you.

22 Redeem Israel, O God, out of all his troubles.

[A Psalm of David.]

26:1 Judge me, O LORD; for I have walked in my integrity: I have trusted also in the LORD; therefore I shall not slide.

2 Examine me, O LORD, and prove me; try my reins and my heart.

3 For your lovingkindness is before my eyes: and I have walked in your truth.

4 I have not sat with vain persons, neither will I go in with dissemblers.

5 I have hated the congregation of evil doers; and will not sit with the wicked.

6 I will wash my hands in innocency: so will I compass your altar, O LORD:

7 That I may publish with the voice of thanksgiving, and tell of all your wondrous works.

8 LORD, I have loved the habitation of your

house, and the place where your honor dwells.

9 Gather not my soul with sinners,
nor my life with bloody men:

10 In whose hands is mischief, and
their right hand is full of bribes.

11 But as for me, I will walk in my integrity:
redeem me, and be merciful to me.

12 My foot stands in an even place: in the
congregations will I bless the LORD.

[A Psalm of David.]

27 **:1** The LORD is my light and my salvation;
whom shall I fear? the LORD is the
strength of my life; of whom shall I be afraid?
2 When the wicked, even my enemies
and my foes, came upon me to eat up
my flesh, they stumbled and fell.

3 Though a host should encamp against me,
my heart shall not fear: though war should
rise against me, in this will I be confident.

4 One thing have I desired of the LORD,
that will I seek after; that I may dwell
in the house of the LORD all the days
of my life, to behold the beauty of the
LORD, and to inquire in his temple.

5 For in the time of trouble he shall hide me in
his pavilion: in the secret of his tabernacle shall

he hide me; he shall set me up upon a rock.

6 And now shall my head be lifted up above my enemies round about me: therefore will I offer in his tabernacle sacrifices of joy; I will sing, yea, I will sing praises to the LORD.

7 Hear, O LORD, when I cry with my voice: have mercy also upon me, and answer me.

8 When you said, *Seek you*[p] *my face;* my heart said to you, Your face, LORD, will I seek.

9 Hide not your face far from me; put not your servant away in anger: you have been my help; leave me not, neither forsake me, O God of my salvation.

10 When my father and my mother forsake me, then the LORD will take me up.

11 Teach me your way, O LORD, and lead me in a plain path, because of my enemies.

12 Deliver me not over to the will of my enemies: for false witnesses are risen up against me, and such as breathe out cruelty.

13 I had fainted, unless I had believed to see the goodness of the LORD in the land of the living.

14 Wait on the LORD: be of good courage, and he shall strengthen your heart: wait, I say, on the LORD.

PSALM 28

[A Psalm of David.]

28:1 Unto you will I cry, O LORD my rock; be not silent to me: lest, if you be silent to me, I become like them that go down into the pit.

2 Hear the voice of my supplications, when I cry to you, when I lift up my hands toward your holy oracle.

3 Draw me not away with the wicked, and with the workers of iniquity, which speak peace to their neighbors, but mischief is in their hearts.

4 Give them according to their deeds, and according to the wickedness of their endeavours: give them after the work of their hands; render to them their desert.

5 Because they regard not the works of the LORD, nor the operation of his hands, he shall destroy them, and not build them up.

6 Blessed be the LORD, because he has heard the voice of my supplications.

7 The LORD is my strength and my shield; my heart trusted in him, and I am helped: therefore my heart greatly rejoices; and with my song will I praise him.

8 The LORD is their strength, and he is the saving strength of his anointed.

Books of the Bible—Psalms

9 Save your people, and bless your inheritance: feed them also, and lift them up for ever.

[A Psalm of David.]

29 :**1** Give to the LORD, O you[p] mighty, give to the LORD glory and strength.
2 Give to the LORD the glory due to his name; worship the LORD in the beauty of holiness.
3 The voice of the LORD is upon the waters: the God of glory thunders: the LORD is upon many waters.
4 The voice of the LORD is powerful; the voice of the LORD is full of majesty.
5 The voice of the LORD breaks the cedars; yea, the LORD breaks the cedars of Lebanon.
6 He makes them also to skip like a calf; Lebanon and Sirion like a young unicorn.
7 The voice of the LORD divides the flames of fire.
8 The voice of the LORD shakes the wilderness; the LORD shakes the wilderness of Kadesh.
9 The voice of the LORD makes the hinds to calve, and discovers the forests: and in his temple does every one speak of his glory.
10 The LORD sits upon the flood; yea, the LORD sits King for ever.
11 The LORD will give strength to his people;

the LORD will bless his people with peace.

[A Psalm and Song at the dedication
of the house of David.]

30:1 I will extol you, O LORD; for you have lifted me up, and have not made my foes to rejoice over me.

2 O LORD my God, I cried to you, and you have healed me.

3 O LORD, you have brought up my soul from the grave: you have kept me alive, that I should not go down to the pit.

4 Sing to the LORD, O you*ᴾ* saints of his, and give thanks at the remembrance of his holiness.

5 For his anger endures but a moment; in his favor is life: weeping may endure for a night, but joy comes in the morning.

6 And in my prosperity I said, I shall never be moved.

7 LORD, by your favor you have made my mountain to stand strong: you did hide your face, and I was troubled.

8 I cried to you, O LORD; and to the LORD I made supplication.

9 What profit is there in my blood, when I go down to the pit? Shall the dust praise you? shall it declare your truth?

10 Hear, O LORD, and have mercy upon me: LORD, be you my helper.

11 You have turned for me my mourning into dancing: you have put off my sackcloth, and girded me with gladness;

12 To the end that my glory may sing praise to you, and not be silent. O LORD my God, I will give thanks to you for ever.

[To the chief Musician, A Psalm of David.]

31:1 In you, O LORD, do I put my trust; let me never be ashamed: deliver me in your righteousness.

2 Bow down your ear to me; deliver me speedily: be you my strong rock, for a house of defense to save me.

3 For you are my rock and my fortress; therefore for your name's sake lead me, and guide me.

4 Pull me out of the net that they have laid privily for me: for you are my strength.

5 Into your hand I commit my spirit: you have redeemed me, O LORD God of truth.

6 I have hated them that regard lying vanities: but I trust in the LORD.

7 I will be glad and rejoice in your mercy: for you have considered my trouble; you have known my soul in adversities;

8 And have not shut me up into the hand of the enemy: you have set my feet in a large room.

9 Have mercy upon me, O LORD, for I am in trouble: my eye is consumed with grief, yea, my soul and my belly.

10 For my life is spent with grief, and my years with sighing: my strength fails because of my iniquity, and my bones are consumed.

11 I was a reproach among all my enemies, but especially among my neighbors, and a fear to my acquaintance: they that did see me outside fled from me.

12 I am forgotten as a dead man out of mind: I am like a broken vessel.

13 For I have heard the slander of many: fear was on every side: while they took counsel together against me, they devised to take away my life.

14 But I trusted in you, O LORD: I said, You are my God.

15 My times are in your hand: deliver me from the hand of my enemies, and from them that persecute me.

16 Make your face to shine upon your servant: save me for your mercies' sake.

17 Let me not be ashamed, O LORD; for I have called upon you: let the wicked be ashamed, and let them be silent in the grave.

18 Let the lying lips be put to silence; which speak grievous things proudly and contemptuously against the righteous.

19 Oh how great is your goodness, which you have laid up for them that fear you; which you have wrought for them that trust in you before the sons of men!

20 You shall hide them in the secret of your presence from the pride of man: you shall keep them secretly in a pavilion from the strife of tongues.

21 Blessed be the LORD: for he has showed me his marvellous kindness in a strong city.

22 For I said in my haste, I am cut off from before your eyes: nevertheless you heard the voice of my supplications when I cried to you.

23 O love the LORD, all you[p] his saints: for the LORD preserves the faithful, and plentifully rewards the proud doer.

24 Be of good courage, and he shall strengthen your[p] heart, all you[p] that hope in the LORD.

PSALM 32

[A Psalm of David, Maschil.]

32:1 Blessed is he whose transgression is forgiven, whose sin is covered.

2 Blessed is the man to whom the LORD imputes not iniquity, and in whose spirit there is no guile.

3 When I kept silence, my bones waxed old through my roaring all the day long.

4 For day and night your hand was heavy upon me: my moisture is turned into the drought of summer. Selah.

5 I acknowledge my sin to you, and my iniquity have I not hid. I said, I will confess my transgressions to the LORD; and you forgave the iniquity of my sin. Selah.

6 For this shall every one that is godly pray to you in a time when you may be found: surely in the floods of great waters they shall not come nigh to him.

7 You are my hiding place; you shall preserve me from trouble; you shall compass me about with songs of deliverance. Selah.

8 I will instruct you and teach you in the way which you shall go: I will guide you with my eye.

9 Be you[P] not as the horse, or as the mule, which have no understanding: whose mouth must be held in with bit and bridle, lest they come near to you.

10 Many sorrows shall be to the wicked: but he that trusts in the LORD, mercy shall compass him about.

11 Be glad in the LORD, and rejoice, you[P] righteous: and shout for joy, all you[P] that are upright in heart.

33 :1 Rejoice in the LORD, O you[P] righteous: for praise is comely for the upright.

2 Praise the LORD with harp: sing to him with the psaltery and an instrument of ten strings.

3 Sing to him a new song; play skillfully with a loud noise.

4 For the word of the LORD is right; and all his works are done in truth.

5 He loves righteousness and judgment: the earth is full of the goodness of the LORD.

6 By the word of the LORD were the heavens made; and all the host of them by the breath of his mouth.

7 He gathers the waters of the sea together as a heap: he lays up the depth in storehouses.

8 Let all the earth fear the LORD: let all the inhabitants of the world stand in awe of him.

9 For he spoke, and it was done; he commanded, and it stood fast.

10 The LORD brings the counsel of
the heathen to nought: he makes the
devices of the people of none effect.

11 The counsel of the LORD stands for ever,
the thoughts of his heart to all generations.

12 Blessed is the nation whose God is
the LORD; and the people whom he
has chosen for his own inheritance.

13 The LORD looks from heaven; he
beholds all the sons of men.

14 From the place of his habitation he looks
upon all the inhabitants of the earth.

15 He fashions their hearts alike;
he considers all their works.

16 There is no king saved by the
multitude of a host: a mighty man is
not delivered by much strength.

17 A horse is a vain thing for safety: neither
shall he deliver any by his great strength.

18 Behold, the eye of the LORD
is upon them that fear him, upon
them that hope in his mercy;

19 To deliver their soul from death,
and to keep them alive in famine.

20 Our soul waits for the LORD: he
is our help and our shield.

21 For our heart shall rejoice in him, because we have trusted in his holy name.

22 Let your mercy, O LORD, be upon us, according as we hope in you.

[A Psalm of David, when he changed his behavior before Abimelech; who drove him away, and he departed.]

34 **:1** I will bless the LORD at all times: his praise shall continually be in my mouth.

2 My soul shall make her boast in the LORD: the humble shall hear thereof, and be glad.

3 O magnify the LORD with me, and let us exalt his name together.

4 I sought the LORD, and he heard me, and delivered me from all my fears.

5 They looked to him, and were lightened: and their faces were not ashamed.

6 This poor man cried, and the LORD heard him, and saved him out of all his troubles.

7 The angel of the LORD encamps round about them that fear him, and delivers them.

8 O taste and see that the LORD is good: blessed is the man that trusts in him.

9 O fear the LORD, you[p] his saints: for there is no want to them that fear him.

10 The young lions do lack, and suffer

hunger: but they that seek the LORD
shall not want any good thing.

11 Come, you[P] children, hearken to me: I
will teach you[P] the fear of the LORD.

12 What man is he that desires life, and
loves many days, that he may see good?

13 Keep your tongue from evil, and
your lips from speaking guile.

14 Depart from evil, and do good;
seek peace, and pursue it.

15 The eyes of the LORD are upon the
righteous, and his ears are open to their cry.

16 The face of the LORD is against
them that do evil, to cut off the
remembrance of them from the earth.

17 The righteous cry, and the LORD hears,
and delivers them out of all their troubles.

18 The LORD is nigh to them that
are of a broken heart; and saves
such as be of a contrite spirit.

19 Many are the afflictions of the righteous:
but the LORD delivers him out of them all.

20 He keeps all his bones: not
one of them is broken.

21 Evil shall slay the wicked: and they that
hate the righteous shall be desolate.

22 The LORD redeems the soul of
his servants: and none of them that
trust in him shall be desolate.

[A Psalm of David.]

35 :1 Plead my cause, O LORD, with
them that strive with me: fight
against them that fight against me.
2 Take hold of shield and buckler,
and stand up for my help.
3 Draw out also the spear, and stop the
way against them that persecute me:
say to my soul, I am your salvation.
4 Let them be confounded and put to shame
that seek after my soul: let them be turned back
and brought to confusion that devise my hurt.
5 Let them be as chaff before the wind: and
let the angel of the LORD chase them.
6 Let their way be dark and slippery: and let
the angel of the LORD persecute them.
7 For without cause have they hid for
me their net in a pit, which without
cause they have dug for my soul.
8 Let destruction come upon him at unawares;
and let his net that he has hid catch himself:
into that very destruction let him fall.
9 And my soul shall be joyful in the

LORD: it shall rejoice in his salvation.

10 All my bones shall say, LORD, who is like to you, which delivers the poor from him that is too strong for him, yea, the poor and the needy from him that spoils him?

11 False witnesses did rise up; they laid to my charge things that I knew not.

12 They rewarded me evil for good to the spoiling of my soul.

13 But as for me, when they were sick, my clothing was sackcloth: I humbled my soul with fasting; and my prayer returned into my own bosom.

14 I behaved myself as though he had been my friend or brother: I bowed down heavily, as one that mourns for his mother.

15 But in my adversity they rejoiced, and gathered themselves together: yea, the abjects gathered themselves together against me, and I knew it not; they did tear me, and ceased not:

16 With hypocritical mockers in feasts, they gnashed upon me with their teeth.

17 Lord, how long will you look on? rescue my soul from their destructions, my darling from the lions.

18 I will give you thanks in the great congregation: I will praise you among much people.

19 Let not them that are my enemies wrongfully
rejoice over me: neither let them wink with
the eye that hate me without a cause.

20 For they speak not peace: but
they devise deceitful matters against
them that are quiet in the land.

21 Yea, they opened their mouth wide against
me, and said, Aha, aha, our eye has seen it.

22 This you have seen, O LORD: keep not
silence: O Lord, be not far from me.

23 Stir up yourself, and awake to my judgment,
even to my cause, my God and my Lord.

24 Judge me, O LORD my God,
according to your righteousness; and
let them not rejoice over me.

25 Let them not say in their hearts,
Ah, so would we have it: let them not
say, We have swallowed him up.

26 Let them be ashamed and brought to
confusion together that rejoice at my hurt:
let them be clothed with shame and dishonor
that magnify themselves against me.

27 Let them shout for joy, and be glad, that
favor my righteous cause: yea, let them say
continually, Let the LORD be magnified, which
has pleasure in the prosperity of his servant.

28 And my tongue shall speak of your righteousness and of your praise all the day long.

[To the chief Musician, A Psalm of David the servant of the LORD.]

36 :1 The transgression of the wicked says within my heart, that there is no fear of God before his eyes.

2 For he flatters himself in his own eyes, until his iniquity be found to be hateful.

3 The words of his mouth are iniquity and deceit: he has left off to be wise, and to do good.

4 He devises mischief upon his bed; he sets himself in a way that is not good; he abhors not evil.

5 Your mercy, O LORD, is in the heavens; and your faithfulness reaches to the clouds.

6 Your righteousness is like the great mountains; your judgments are a great deep: O LORD, you preserve man and beast.

7 How excellent is your lovingkindness, O God! therefore the children of men put their trust under the shadow of your wings.

8 They shall be abundantly satisfied with the fatness of your house; and you shall make them drink of the river of your pleasures.

9 For with you is the fountain of life:
in your light shall we see light.

10 O continue your lovingkindness
to them that know you; and your
righteousness to the upright in heart.

11 Let not the foot of pride come against me,
and let not the hand of the wicked remove me.

12 There are the workers of iniquity fallen: they
are cast down, and shall not be able to rise.

[A Psalm of David.]

37:1 Fret not yourself because of
evildoers, neither be you envious
against the workers of iniquity.

2 For they shall soon be cut down like the
grass, and wither as the green herb.

3 Trust in the LORD, and do good; so shall you
dwell in the land, and verily you shall be fed.

4 Delight yourself also in the LORD: and he
shall give you the desires of your heart.

5 Commit your way to the LORD; trust also
in him; and he shall bring it to pass.

6 And he shall bring forth your righteousness as
the light, and your judgment as the noonday.

7 Rest in the LORD, and wait patiently for
him: fret not yourself because of him who

prospers in his way, because of the man who brings wicked devices to pass.

8 Cease from anger, and forsake wrath: fret not yourself in any wise to do evil.

9 For evildoers shall be cut off: but those that wait upon the LORD, they shall inherit the earth.

10 For yet a little while, and the wicked shall not be: yea, you shall diligently consider his place, and it shall not be.

11 But the meek shall inherit the earth; and shall delight themselves in the abundance of peace.

12 The wicked plots against the just, and gnashes upon him with his teeth.

13 The Lord shall laugh at him: for he sees that his day is coming.

14 The wicked have drawn out the sword, and have bent their bow, to cast down the poor and needy, and to slay such as be of upright conversation.

15 Their sword shall enter into their own heart, and their bows shall be broken.

16 A little that a righteous man has is better than the riches of many wicked.

17 For the arms of the wicked shall be broken: but the LORD upholds the righteous.

18 The LORD knows the days of the upright:

and their inheritance shall be for ever.

19 They shall not be ashamed in the evil time: and in the days of famine they shall be satisfied.

20 But the wicked shall perish, and the enemies of the LORD shall be as the fat of lambs: they shall consume; into smoke shall they consume away.

21 The wicked borrows, and pays not again: but the righteous shows mercy, and gives.

22 For such as be blessed of him shall inherit the earth; and they that be cursed of him shall be cut off.

23 The steps of a good man are ordered by the LORD: and he delights in his way.

24 Though he fall, he shall not be utterly cast down: for the LORD upholds him with his hand.

25 I have been young, and now am old; yet have I not seen the righteous forsaken, nor his seed begging bread.

26 He is ever merciful, and lends; and his seed is blessed.

27 Depart from evil, and do good; and dwell for evermore.

28 For the LORD loves judgment, and forsakes not his saints; they are preserved for ever: but the seed of the wicked shall be cut off.

PSALM 37

29 The righteous shall inherit the land, and dwell therein for ever.

30 The mouth of the righteous speaks wisdom, and his tongue talks of judgment.

31 The law of his God is in his heart; none of his steps shall slide.

32 The wicked watches the righteous, and seeks to slay him.

33 The LORD will not leave him in his hand, nor condemn him when he is judged.

34 Wait on the LORD, and keep his way, and he shall exalt you to inherit the land: when the wicked are cut off, you shall see it.

35 I have seen the wicked in great power, and spreading himself like a green bay tree.

36 Yet he passed away, and, lo, he was not: yea, I sought him, but he could not be found.

37 Mark the perfect man, and behold the upright: for the end of that man is peace.

38 But the transgressors shall be destroyed together: the end of the wicked shall be cut off.

39 But the salvation of the righteous is of the LORD: he is their strength in the time of trouble.

40 And the LORD shall help them, and deliver them: he shall deliver them from the wicked, and save them, because they trust in him.

Books of the Bible—Psalms

[A Psalm of David, to bring to remembrance.]

38 :1 O LORD, rebuke me not in your wrath: neither chasten me in your hot displeasure.

2 For your arrows stick fast in me, and your hand presses me sore.

3 There is no soundness in my flesh because of your anger; neither is there any rest in my bones because of my sin.

4 For my iniquities are gone over my head: as a heavy burden they are too heavy for me.

5 My wounds stink and are corrupt because of my foolishness.

6 I am troubled; I am bowed down greatly; I go mourning all the day long.

7 For my loins are filled with a loathsome disease: and there is no soundness in my flesh.

8 I am feeble and sore broken: I have roared by reason of the disquietness of my heart.

9 Lord, all my desire is before you; and my groaning is not hid from you.

10 My heart pants, my strength fails me: as for the light of my eyes, it also is gone from me.

11 My lovers and my friends stand aloof from my sore; and my kinsmen stand afar off.

12 They also that seek after my life lay

snares for me: and they that seek my hurt speak mischievous things, and imagine deceits all the day long.

13 But I, as a deaf man, heard not; and I was as a dumb man that opens not his mouth.

14 Thus I was as a man that hears not, and in whose mouth are no reproofs.

15 For in you, O LORD, do I hope: you will hear, O Lord my God.

16 For I said, Hear me, lest otherwise they should rejoice over me: when my foot slips, they magnify themselves against me.

17 For I am ready to halt, and my sorrow is continually before me.

18 For I will declare my iniquity; I will be sorry for my sin.

19 But my enemies are lively, and they are strong: and they that hate me wrongfully are multiplied.

20 They also that render evil for good are my adversaries; because I follow the thing that good is.

21 Forsake me not, O LORD: O my God, be not far from me.

22 Make haste to help me, O Lord my salvation.

[To the chief Musician, even to Jeduthun, A Psalm of David.]

39:1 I said, I will take heed to my ways, that I sin not with my tongue: I will keep my mouth with a bridle, while the wicked is before me.

2 I was dumb with silence, I held my peace, even from good; and my sorrow was stirred.

3 My heart was hot within me, while I was musing the fire burned: then spoke I with my tongue,

4 LORD, make me to know my end, and the measure of my days, what it is: that I may know how frail I am.

5 Behold, you have made my days as a handbreadth; and my age is as nothing before you: verily every man at his best state is altogether vanity. Selah.

6 Surely every man walks in a vain show: surely they are disquieted in vain: he heaps up riches, and knows not who shall gather them.

7 And now, Lord, what wait I for? my hope is in you.

8 Deliver me from all my transgressions: make me not the reproach of the foolish.

9 I was dumb, I opened not my mouth; because you did it.

10 Remove your stroke away from me: I am consumed by the blow of your hand.

11 When you with rebukes do correct man for iniquity, you make his beauty to consume away like a moth: surely every man is vanity. Selah.

12 Hear my prayer, O LORD, and give ear to my cry; hold not your peace at my tears: for I am a stranger with you, and a sojourner, as all my fathers were.

13 O spare me, that I may recover strength, before I go from here, and be no more.

[To the chief Musician, A Psalm of David.]

40:1 I waited patiently for the LORD; and he inclined to me, and heard my cry.

2 He brought me up also out of a horrible pit, out of the miry clay, and set my feet upon a rock, and established my goings.

3 And he has put a new song in my mouth, even praise to our God: many shall see it, and fear, and shall trust in the LORD.

4 Blessed is that man that makes the LORD his trust, and respects not the proud, nor such as turn aside to lies.

5 Many, O LORD my God, are your wonderful works which you have done, and your thoughts which are to us-ward: they cannot be reckoned up in order to you: if I would declare and speak of them, they are more than can be numbered.

6 Sacrifice and offering you did not desire; my ears have you opened: burnt offering and sin offering have you not required.

7 Then said I, Lo, I come: in the volume of the book it is written of me,

8 I delight to do your will, O my God: yea, your law is within my heart.

9 I have preached righteousness in the great congregation: lo, I have not refrained my lips, O LORD, you know.

10 I have not hid your righteousness within my heart; I have declared your faithfulness and your salvation: I have not concealed your lovingkindness and your truth from the great congregation.

11 Withhold not you your tender mercies from me, O LORD: let your lovingkindness and your truth continually preserve me.

12 For innumerable evils have compassed me about: my iniquities have taken hold upon me, so that I am not able to look up; they are more than the hairs of my head: therefore my heart fails me.

13 Be pleased, O LORD, to deliver me: O LORD, make haste to help me.

14 Let them be ashamed and confounded together that seek after my soul to destroy it; let them be driven backward and put to shame that wish me evil.

15 Let them be desolate for a reward of their shame that say to me, Aha, aha.

16 Let all those that seek you rejoice and be glad in you: let such as love your salvation say continually, The LORD be magnified.

17 But I am poor and needy; yet the Lord thinks upon me: you are my help and my deliverer; make no tarrying, O my God.

[To the chief Musician, A Psalm of David.]

41 **:1** Blessed is he that considers the poor: the LORD will deliver him in time of trouble.
2 The LORD will preserve him, and keep him alive; and he shall be blessed upon the earth: and you will not deliver him to the will of his enemies.

3 The LORD will strengthen him upon the bed of languishing: you will make all his bed in his sickness.

4 I said, LORD, be merciful to me: heal my soul; for I have sinned against you.

5 My enemies speak evil of me, When shall he die, and his name perish?

6 And if he come to see me, he speaks vanity: his heart gathers iniquity to itself; when he goes abroad, he tells it.

7 All that hate me whisper together against me: against me do they devise my hurt.

8 An evil disease, say they, cleaves fast to him: and now that he lies he shall rise up no more.

9 Yea, my own familiar friend, in whom I trusted, which did eat of my bread, has lifted up his heel against me.

10 But you, O LORD, be merciful to me, and raise me up, that I may requite them.

11 By this I know that you favor me, because my enemy does not triumph over me.

12 And as for me, you uphold me in my integrity, and set me before your face for ever.

13 Blessed be the LORD God of Israel from everlasting, and to everlasting. Amen, and Amen.

[To the chief Musician, Maschil, for the sons of Korah.]

42 **:1** As the hart pants after the water brooks, so pants my soul after you, O God.

2 My soul thirsts for God, for the living God: when shall I come and appear before God?

3 My tears have been my meat day

and night, while they continually say
to me, Where is your God?

4 When I remember these things, I pour
out my soul in me: for I had gone with the
multitude, I went with them to the house
of God, with the voice of joy and praise,
with a multitude that kept holyday.

5 Why are you cast down, O my soul?
and why are you disquieted in me? hope
you in God: for I shall yet praise him
for the help of his countenance.

6 O my God, my soul is cast down
within me: therefore will I remember
you from the land of Jordan, and of the
Hermonites, from the hill Mizar.

7 Deep calls to deep at the noise of
your waterspouts: all your waves and
your billows are gone over me.

8 Yet the LORD will command his
lovingkindness in the day time, and in
the night his song shall be with me, and
my prayer to the God of my life.

9 I will say to God my rock, Why have
you forgotten me? why go I mourning
because of the oppression of the enemy?

10 As with a sword in my bones, my
enemies reproach me; while they say

RenewingLives.com

daily to me, Where is your God?

11 Why are you cast down, O my soul? and why are you disquieted within me? hope you in God: for I shall yet praise him, who is the health of my countenance, and my God.

43 :1 Judge me, O God, and plead my cause against an ungodly nation: O deliver me from the deceitful and unjust man.

2 For you are the God of my strength: why do you cast me off? why go I mourning because of the oppression of the enemy?

3 O send out your light and your truth: let them lead me; let them bring me to your holy hill, and to your tabernacles.

4 Then will I go to the altar of God, to God my exceeding joy: yes, upon the harp will I praise you, O God my God.

5 Why are you cast down, O my soul? and why are you disquieted within me? hope in God: for I shall yet praise him, who is the health of my countenance, and my God.

[To the chief Musician for the sons of Korah, Maschil.]

44 :1 We have heard with our ears, O God, our fathers have told us, what work you did in their days, in the times of old.

2 How you did drive out the heathen with your hand, and planted them; how you did afflict the people, and cast them out.

3 For they got not the land in possession by their own sword, neither did their own arm save them: but your right hand, and your arm, and the light of your countenance, because you had a favor to them.

4 You are my King, O God: command deliverances for Jacob.

5 Through you will we push down our enemies: through your name will we tread them under that rise up against us.

6 For I will not trust in my bow, neither shall my sword save me.

7 But you have saved us from our enemies, and have put them to shame that hated us.

8 In God we boast all the day long, and praise your name for ever. Selah.

9 But you have cast off, and put us to shame; and go not forth with our armies.

10 You make us to turn back from the enemy: and they which hate us spoil for themselves.

11 You have given us like sheep appointed for meat; and have scattered us among the heathen.

12 You sell your people for nought, and do not increase your wealth by their price.

13 You make us a reproach to our neighbors, a scorn and a derision to them that are round about us.

14 You make us a byword among the heathen, a shaking of the head among the people.

15 My confusion is continually before me, and the shame of my face has covered me,

16 For the voice of him that reproaches and blasphemes; by reason of the enemy and avenger.

17 All this is come upon us; yet have we not forgotten you, neither have we dealt falsely in your covenant.

18 Our heart is not turned back, neither have our steps declined from your way;

19 Though you have sore broken us in the place of dragons, and covered us with the shadow of death.

20 If we have forgotten the name of our God, or stretched out our hands to a strange god;

21 Shall not God search this out? for he knows the secrets of the heart.

22 Yes, for your sake are we killed all the day

long; we are counted as sheep for the slaughter.

23 Awake, why sleep you, O Lord?
arise, cast us not off for ever.

24 Wherefore hide you your face, and
forget our affliction and our oppression?

25 For our soul is bowed down to the
dust: our belly cleaves to the earth.

26 Arise for our help, and redeem
us for your mercies' sake.

[To the chief Musician upon Shoshannim, for
the sons of Korah, Maschil, A Song of loves.]

45:1 My heart is inditing a good
matter: I speak of the things which
I have made touching the king: my
tongue is the pen of a ready writer.

2 You are fairer than the children of men:
grace is poured into your lips: therefore
God has blessed you for ever.

3 Gird your sword upon your thigh, O most
mighty, with your glory and your majesty.

4 And in your majesty ride prosperously because
of truth and meekness and righteousness; and
your right hand shall teach you terrible things.

5 Your arrows are sharp in the heart
of the king's enemies; whereby
the people fall under you.

6 Your throne, O God, is for ever and ever: the sceptre of your kingdom is a right sceptre.

7 You love righteousness, and hate wickedness: therefore God, your God, has anointed you with the oil of gladness above your fellows.

8 All your garments smell of myrrh, and aloes, and cassia, out of the ivory palaces, whereby they have made you glad.

9 Kings' daughters were among your honorable women: upon your right hand did stand the queen in gold of Ophir.

10 Hearken, O daughter, and consider, and incline your ear; forget also your own people, and your father's house;

11 So shall the king greatly desire your beauty: for he is your Lord; and worship you him.

12 And the daughter of Tyre shall be there with a gift; even the rich among the people shall entreat your favor.

13 The king's daughter is all glorious within: her clothing is of wrought gold.

14 She shall be brought to the king in raiment of needlework: the virgins her companions that follow her shall be brought to you.

15 With gladness and rejoicing shall they be brought: they shall enter into the king's palace.

16 Instead of your fathers shall be your children, whom you may make princes in all the earth.

17 I will make your name to be remembered in all generations: therefore shall the people praise you for ever and ever.

[To the chief Musician for the sons of Korah, A Song upon Alamoth.]

46 **:1** God is our refuge and strength, a very present help in trouble.

2 Therefore will not we fear, though the earth be removed, and though the mountains be carried into the midst of the sea;

3 Though the waters thereof roar and be troubled, though the mountains shake with the swelling thereof. Selah.

4 There is a river, the streams whereof shall make glad the city of God, the holy place of the tabernacles of the most High.

5 God is in the midst of her; she shall not be moved: God shall help her, and that right early.

6 The heathen raged, the kingdoms were moved: he uttered his voice, the earth melted.

7 The LORD of hosts is with us; the God of Jacob is our refuge. Selah.

8 Come, behold the works of the Lord, what desolations he has made in the earth.

9 He makes wars to cease to the end of the earth; he breaks the bow, and cuts the spear in sunder; he burns the chariot in the fire.

10 *Be still, and know that I am God:*
I will be exalted among the heathen,
I will be exalted in the earth.

11 The LORD of hosts is with us; the God of Jacob is our refuge. Selah.

[To the chief Musician, A Psalm
for the sons of Korah.]

47 **:1** O clap your*ᴾ* hands, all you*ᴾ* people; shout to God with the voice of triumph.

2 For the LORD most high is terrible; he is a great King over all the earth.

3 He shall subdue the people under us, and the nations under our feet.

4 He shall choose our inheritance for us, the excellency of Jacob whom he loved. Selah.

5 God is gone up with a shout, the LORD with the sound of a trumpet.

6 Sing praises to God, sing praises: sing praises to our King, sing praises.

7 For God is the King of all the earth: sing you*ᴾ* praises with understanding.

8 God reigns over the heathen: God sits upon the throne of his holiness.

9 The princes of the people are gathered together, even the people of the God of Abraham: for the shields of the earth belong to God: he is greatly exalted.

[A Song and Psalm for the sons of Korah.]

48:1 Great is the LORD, and greatly to be praised in the city of our God, in the mountain of his holiness.

2 Beautiful for situation, the joy of the whole earth, is mount Zion, on the sides of the north, the city of the great King.

3 God is known in her palaces for a refuge.

4 For, lo, the kings were assembled, they passed by together.

5 They saw it, and so they marvelled; they were troubled, and hasted away.

6 Fear took hold upon them there, and pain, as of a woman in travail.

7 You break the ships of Tarshish with an east wind.

8 As we have heard, so have we seen in the city of the LORD of hosts, in the city of our God: God will establish it for ever. Selah.

9 We have thought of your lovingkindness, O God, in the midst of your temple.

10 According to your name, O God, so is

RenewingLives.com

your praise to the ends of the earth: your
right hand is full of righteousness.

11 Let mount Zion rejoice, let the daughters of
Judah be glad, because of your judgments.

12 Walk about Zion, and go round
about her: tell the towers thereof.

13 Mark you^P well her bulwarks,
consider her palaces; that you^P may
tell it to the generation following.

14 For this God is our God for ever and
ever: he will be our guide even to death.

[To the chief Musician, A Psalm
for the sons of Korah.]

49 :1 Hear this, all you^P people; give ear,
all you^P inhabitants of the world:

2 Both low and high, rich and poor, together.

3 My mouth shall speak of wisdom;
and the meditation of my heart
shall be of understanding.

4 I will incline my ear to a parable: I will
open my dark saying upon the harp.

5 Wherefore should I fear in the
days of evil, when the iniquity of my
heels shall compass me about?

6 They that trust in their wealth, and boast
themselves in the multitude of their riches;

7 None of them can by any means redeem his brother, nor give to God a ransom for him:

8 (For the redemption of their soul is precious, and it ceases for ever:)

9 That he should still live for ever, and not see corruption.

10 For he sees that wise men die, likewise the fool and the brutish person perish, and leave their wealth to others.

11 Their inward thought is, that their houses shall continue for ever, and their dwelling places to all generations; they call their lands after their own names.

12 Nevertheless man being in honor abides not: he is like the beasts that perish.

13 This their way is their folly: yet their posterity approve their sayings. Selah.

14 Like sheep they are laid in the grave; death shall feed on them; and the upright shall have dominion over them in the morning; and their beauty shall consume in the grave from their dwelling.

15 But God will redeem my soul from the power of the grave: for he shall receive me. Selah.

16 Be not you afraid when one is made rich, when the glory of his house is increased;

17 For when he dies he shall carry nothing away: his glory shall not descend after him.

18 Though while he lived he blessed his soul: and men will praise you, when you do well to yourself.

19 He shall go to the generation of his fathers; they shall never see light.

20 Man that is in honor, and understands not, is like the beasts that perish.

[A Psalm of Asaph.]

50 :1 The mighty God, even the LORD, has spoken, and called the earth from the rising of the sun to the going down thereof.
2 Out of Zion, the perfection of beauty, God has shined.

3 Our God shall come, and shall not keep silence: a fire shall devour before him, and it shall be very tempestuous round about him.

4 He shall call to the heavens from above, and to the earth, that he may judge his people.

5 *Gather my saints together to me; those that have made a covenant with me by sacrifice.*

6 And the heavens shall declare his righteousness: for God is judge himself. Selah.

7 *Hear, O my people, and I will speak; O Israel, and I will testify against* *you: I am God, even your God.*

8 *I will not reprove you for your sacrifices or your burnt offerings, to have been continually before me.*

9 *I will take no bullock out of your house, nor he goats out of your folds.*

10 *For every beast of the forest is mine, and the cattle upon a thousand hills.*

11 *I know all the fowls of the mountains: and the wild beasts of the field are mine.*

12 *If I were hungry, I would not tell you: for the world is mine, and the fulness thereof.*

13 *Will I eat the flesh of bulls, or drink the blood of goats?*

14 *Offer to God thanksgiving; and pay your vows to the most High:*

15 *And call upon me in the day of trouble: I will deliver you, and you shall glorify me.*

16 But to the wicked God says, *What have you to do to declare my statutes, or that you should take my covenant in your mouth?*

17 *Seeing you hate instruction, and cast my words behind you.*

18 *When you saw a thief, then you consented with him, and have been partaker with adulterers.*

19 *You give your mouth to evil, and your tongue frames deceit.*

20 *You sit and speak against your brother; you slander your own mother's son.*

21 *These things have you done, and I kept silence; you thought that I was altogether such a one as yourself: but I will reprove you, and set them in order before your eyes.*

22 *Now consider this, you[p] that forget God, lest I tear you[p] in pieces, and there be none to deliver.*

23 *Whoso offers praise glorifies me: and to him that orders his conversation aright will I show the salvation of God.*

[To the chief Musician, A Psalm of David, when Nathan the prophet came to him, after he had gone in to Bathsheba.]

51 :1 Have mercy upon me, O God, according to your lovingkindness: according to the multitude of your tender mercies blot out my transgressions.

2 Wash me throughly from my iniquity, and cleanse me from my sin.

3 For I acknowledge my transgressions: and my sin is ever before me.

4 Against you, you only, have I sinned, and done this evil in your sight: that you might be justified

PSALM 51

when you speak, and be clear when you judge.

5 Behold, I was shapen in iniquity; and in sin did my mother conceive me.

6 Behold, you desire truth in the inward parts: and in the hidden part you shall make me to know wisdom.

7 Purge me with hyssop, and I shall be clean: wash me, and I shall be whiter than snow.

8 Make me to hear joy and gladness; that the bones which you have broken may rejoice.

9 Hide your face from my sins, and blot out all my iniquities.

10 Create in me a clean heart, O God; and renew a right spirit within me.

11 Cast me not away from your presence; and take not your holy spirit from me.

12 Restore to me the joy of your salvation; and uphold me with your free spirit.

13 Then will I teach transgressors your ways; and sinners shall be converted to you.

14 Deliver me from bloodguiltiness, O God, you God of my salvation: and my tongue shall sing aloud of your righteousness.

15 O Lord, open you my lips; and my mouth shall show forth your praise.

16 For you desire not sacrifice; else would I

give it: you delight not in burnt offering.

17 The sacrifices of God are a broken spirit: a broken and a contrite heart, O God, you will not despise.

18 Do good in your good pleasure to Zion: build you the walls of Jerusalem.

19 Then shall you be pleased with the sacrifices of righteousness, with burnt offering and whole burnt offering: then shall they offer bullocks upon your altar.

[To the chief Musician, Maschil, A Psalm of David, when Doeg the Edomite came and told Saul, and said to him, David is come to the house of Ahimelech.]

52 :1 Why boast you yourself in mischief, O mighty man? the goodness of God endures continually.

2 The tongue devises mischiefs; like a sharp razor, working deceitfully.

3 You love evil more than good; and lying rather than to speak righteousness. Selah.

4 You love all devouring words, O you deceitful tongue.

5 God shall likewise destroy you for ever, he shall take you away, and pluck you out of your dwelling place, and root you out of the land of the living. Selah.

6 The righteous also shall see, and fear, and shall laugh at him:

7 Lo, this is the man that made not God his strength; but trusted in the abundance of his riches, and strengthened himself in his wickedness.

8 But I am like a green olive tree in the house of God: I trust in the mercy of God for ever and ever.

9 I will praise you for ever, because you have done it: and I will wait on your name; for it is good before your saints.

[To the chief Musician upon Mahalath, Maschil, A Psalm of David.]

53:1 The fool has said in his heart, There is no God. Corrupt are they, and have done abominable iniquity: there is none that does good.

2 God looked down from heaven upon the children of men, to see if there were any that did understand, that did seek God.

3 Every one of them is gone back: they are altogether become filthy; there is none that does good, no, not one.

4 Have the workers of iniquity no knowledge?

who eat up my people as they eat bread:
they have not called upon God.

5 There were they in great fear, where no fear
was: for God has scattered the bones of him
that encamps against you: you have put them
to shame, because God has despised them.

6 Oh that the salvation of Israel were
come out of Zion! When God brings back
the captivity of his people, Jacob shall
rejoice, and Israel shall be glad.

[To the chief Musician on Neginoth, Maschil, A
Psalm of David, when the Ziphims came and said
to Saul, Does not David hide himself with us?]

54 :1 Save me, O God, by your name,
and judge me by your strength.

2 Hear my prayer, O God; give ear
to the words of my mouth.

3 For strangers are risen up against me,
and oppressors seek after my soul: they
have not set God before them. Selah.

4 Behold, God is my helper: the Lord
is with them that uphold my soul.

5 He shall reward evil to my enemies:
cut them off in your truth.

6 I will freely sacrifice to you: I will praise
your name, O LORD; for it is good.

7 For he has delivered me out of all trouble: and my eye has seen his desire upon my enemies.

[To the chief Musician on Neginoth, Maschil, A Psalm of David.]

55:**1** Give ear to my prayer, O God; and hide not yourself from my supplication.

2 Attend to me, and hear me: I mourn in my complaint, and make a noise;

3 Because of the voice of the enemy, because of the oppression of the wicked: for they cast iniquity upon me, and in wrath they hate me.

4 My heart is sore pained within me: and the terrors of death are fallen upon me.

5 Fearfulness and trembling are come upon me, and horror has overwhelmed me.

6 And I said, Oh that I had wings like a dove! for then would I fly away, and be at rest.

7 Lo, then would I wander far off, and remain in the wilderness. Selah.

8 I would hasten my escape from the windy storm and tempest.

9 Destroy, O Lord, and divide their tongues: for I have seen violence and strife in the city.

10 Day and night they go about it upon the walls thereof: mischief also and sorrow are in the midst of it.

11 Wickedness is in the midst thereof: deceit and guile depart not from her streets.

12 For it was not an enemy that reproached me; then I could have borne it: neither was it he that hated me that did magnify himself against me; then I would have hid myself from him:

13 But it was you, a man my equal, my guide, and my acquaintance.

14 We took sweet counsel together, and walked to the house of God in company.

15 Let death seize upon them, and let them go down quick into hell: for wickedness is in their dwellings, and among them.

16 As for me, I will call upon God; and the LORD shall save me.

17 Evening, and morning, and at noon, will I pray, and cry aloud: and he shall hear my voice.

18 He has delivered my soul in peace from the battle that was against me: for there were many with me.

19 God shall hear, and afflict them, even he that abides of old. Selah. Because they have no changes, therefore they fear not God.

20 He has put forth his hands against such as be at peace with him: he has broken his covenant.

21 The words of his mouth were smoother than

butter, but war was in his heart: his words were softer than oil, yet were they drawn swords.

22 Cast your burden upon the LORD, and he shall sustain you: he shall never suffer the righteous to be moved.

23 But you, O God, shall bring them down into the pit of destruction: bloody and deceitful men shall not live out half their days; but I will trust in you.

[To the chief Musician upon Jonathelemrechokim, Michtam of David, when the Philistines took him in Gath.]

56 :1 Be merciful to me, O God: for man would swallow me up; he fighting daily oppresses me.

2 My enemies would daily swallow me up: for they be many that fight against me, O you most High.

3 What time I am afraid, I will trust in you.

4 In God I will praise his word, in God I have put my trust; I will not fear what flesh can do to me.

5 Every day they wrest my words: all their thoughts are against me for evil.

6 They gather themselves together, they hide themselves, they mark my steps, when they wait for my soul.

7 Shall they escape by iniquity? in your anger cast down the people, O God.

8 You tell my wanderings: put you my tears into your bottle: are they not in your book?

9 When I cry to you, then shall my enemies turn back: this I know; for God is for me.

10 In God will I praise his word: in the LORD will I praise his word.

11 In God have I put my trust: I will not be afraid what man can do to me.

12 Your vows are upon me, O God: I will render praises to you.

13 For you have delivered my soul from death: will not you deliver my feet from falling, that I may walk before God in the light of the living?

[To the chief Musician, Altaschith, Michtam of David, when he fled from Saul in the cave.]

57 :1 Be merciful to me, O God, be merciful to me: for my soul trusts in you: yes, in the shadow of your wings will I make my refuge, until these calamities be overpast.

2 I will cry to God most high; to God that performs all things for me.

3 He shall send from heaven, and save me from the reproach of him that would swallow me up. Selah. God shall send forth his mercy and his truth.

4 My soul is among lions: and I lie even among them that are set on fire, even the sons of men, whose teeth are spears and arrows, and their tongue a sharp sword.

5 Be you exalted, O God, above the heavens; let your glory be above all the earth.

6 They have prepared a net for my steps; my soul is bowed down: they have dug a pit before me, into the midst whereof they are fallen themselves. Selah.

7 My heart is fixed, O God, my heart is fixed: I will sing and give praise.

8 Awake up, my glory; awake, psaltery and harp: I myself will awake early.

9 I will praise you, O Lord, among the people: I will sing to you among the nations.

10 For your mercy is great to the heavens, and your truth to the clouds.

11 Be you exalted, O God, above the heavens: let your glory be above all the earth.

[To the chief Musician, Altaschith, Michtam of David.]

58 :1 Do you[p] indeed speak righteousness, O congregation? do you[p] judge uprightly, O you[p] sons of men?

2 Yes, in heart you[P] work wickedness; you[P] weigh the violence of your[P] hands in the earth.

3 The wicked are estranged from the womb: they go astray as soon as they be born, speaking lies.

4 Their poison is like the poison of a serpent: they are like the deaf adder that stops her ear;

5 Which will not hearken to the voice of charmers, charming never so wisely.

6 Break their teeth, O God, in their mouth: break out the great teeth of the young lions, O LORD.

7 Let them melt away as waters which run continually: when he bends his bow to shoot his arrows, let them be as cut in pieces.

8 As a snail which melts, let every one of them pass away: like the untimely birth of a woman, that they may not see the sun.

9 Before your[P] pots can feel the thorns, he shall take them away as with a whirlwind, both living, and in his wrath.

10 The righteous shall rejoice when he sees the vengeance: he shall wash his feet in the blood of the wicked.

11 So that a man shall say, Verily there is a reward for the righteous: verily he is a God that judges in the earth.

PSALM 59

[To the chief Musician, Altaschith, Michtam of David; when Saul sent, and they watched the house to kill him.]

59 :1 Deliver me from my enemies, O my God: defend me from them that rise up against me.

2 Deliver me from the workers of iniquity, and save me from bloody men.

3 For, lo, they lie in wait for my soul: the mighty are gathered against me; not for my transgression, nor for my sin, O LORD.

4 They run and prepare themselves without my fault: awake to help me, and behold.

5 You therefore, O LORD God of hosts, the God of Israel, awake to visit all the heathen: be not merciful to any wicked transgressors. Selah.

6 They return at evening: they make a noise like a dog, and go round about the city.

7 Behold, they belch out with their mouth: swords are in their lips: for who, say they, does hear?

8 But you, O LORD, shall laugh at them; you shall have all the heathen in derision.

9 Because of his strength will I wait upon you: for God is my defense.

10 The God of my mercy shall prevent me: God

Books of the Bible—Psalms

shall let me see my desire upon my enemies.

11 Slay them not, lest my people forget:
scatter them by your power; and bring
them down, O Lord our shield.

12 For the sin of their mouth and the words of
their lips let them even be taken in their pride:
and for cursing and lying which they speak.

13 Consume them in wrath, consume them, that
they may not be: and let them know that God
rules in Jacob to the ends of the earth. Selah.

14 And at evening let them return;
and let them make a noise like a dog,
and go round about the city.

15 Let them wander up and down for meat,
and grudge if they be not satisfied.

16 But I will sing of your power; yes,
I will sing aloud of your mercy in the
morning: for you have been my defense
and refuge in the day of my trouble.

17 Unto you, O my strength, will I sing: for God
is my defense, and the God of my mercy.

PSALM 60

[To the chief Musician upon Shushaneduth, Michtam of David, to teach; when he strove with Aramnaharaim and with Aramzobah, when Joab returned, and smote of Edom in the valley of salt twelve thousand.]

60:1 O God, you have cast us off, you have scattered us, you have been displeased; O turn yourself to us again.

2 You have made the earth to tremble; you have broken it: heal the breaches thereof; for it shakes.

3 You have showed your people hard things: you have made us to drink the wine of astonishment.

4 You have given a banner to them that fear you, that it may be displayed because of the truth. Selah.

5 That your beloved may be delivered; save with your right hand, and hear me.

6 God has spoken in his holiness; *I will rejoice, I will divide Shechem, and mete out the valley of Succoth.*

7 *Gilead is mine, and Manasseh is mine; Ephraim also is the strength of my head; Judah is my lawgiver;*

8 *Moab is my washpot; over Edom will I cast out my shoe: Philistia, triumph you because of me.*

9 Who will bring me into the strong

Books of the Bible—Psalms

city? who will lead me into Edom?

10 Will not you, O God, which had
cast us off? and you, O God, which
did not go out with our armies?

11 Give us help from trouble: for
vain is the help of man.

12 Through God we shall do valiantly: for he
it is that shall tread down our enemies.

[To the chief Musician upon
Neginah, A Psalm of David.]

61:**1** Hear my cry, O God; attend to my prayer.
2 From the end of the earth will I cry
to you, when my heart is overwhelmed:
lead me to the rock that is higher than I.

3 For you have been a shelter for me,
and a strong tower from the enemy.

4 I will abide in your tabernacle for ever: I
will trust in the covert of your wings. Selah.

5 For you, O God, have heard my
vows: you have given me the heritage
of those that fear your name.

6 You will prolong the king's life: and
his years as many generations.

7 He shall abide before God for ever: O prepare
mercy and truth, which may preserve him.

8 So will I sing praise to your name for ever,

that I may daily perform my vows.

[To the chief Musician, to Jeduthun,
A Psalm of David.]

62:1 Truly my soul waits upon God:
from him comes my salvation.

2 He only is my rock and my salvation; he is my defense; I shall not be greatly moved.

3 How long will you*P* imagine mischief against a man? you*P* shall be slain all of you*P*: as a bowing wall shall you*P* be, and as a tottering fence.

4 They only consult to cast him down from his excellency: they delight in lies: they bless with their mouth, but they curse inwardly. Selah.

5 My soul, wait you only upon God;
for my expectation is from him.

6 He only is my rock and my salvation: he is my defense; I shall not be moved.

7 In God is my salvation and my glory: the rock of my strength, and my refuge, is in God.

8 Trust in him at all times; you*P* people,
pour out your*P* heart before him:
God is a refuge for us. Selah.

9 Surely men of low degree are vanity, and men of high degree are a lie: to be laid in the balance, they are altogether lighter than vanity.

10 Trust not in oppression, and become

not vain in robbery: if riches increase,
set not your[p] heart upon them.

11 God has spoken once; twice have I
heard this; that power belongs to God.

12 Also to you, O Lord, belongs mercy: for you
render to every man according to his work.

[A Psalm of David, when he was
in the wilderness of Judah.]

63:1 O God, you are my God; early
will I seek you: my soul thirsts
for you, my flesh longs for you in a dry
and thirsty land, where no water is;

2 To see your power and your glory, so
as I have seen you in the sanctuary.

3 Because your lovingkindness is better
than life, my lips shall praise you.

4 Thus will I bless you while I live: I
will lift up my hands in your name.

5 My soul shall be satisfied as with
marrow and fatness; and my mouth
shall praise you with joyful lips:

6 When I remember you upon my bed, and
meditate on you in the night watches.

7 Because you have been my help, therefore
in the shadow of your wings will I rejoice.

8 My soul follows hard after you:

your right hand upholds me.

9 But those that seek my soul, to destroy it, shall go into the lower parts of the earth.

10 They shall fall by the sword: they shall be a portion for foxes.

11 But the king shall rejoice in God; every one that swears by him shall glory: but the mouth of them that speak lies shall be stopped.

[To the chief Musician, A Psalm of David.]

64:1 Hear my voice, O God, in my prayer: preserve my life from fear of the enemy.

2 Hide me from the secret counsel of the wicked; from the insurrection of the workers of iniquity:

3 Who whet their tongue like a sword, and bend their bows to shoot their arrows, even bitter words:

4 That they may shoot in secret at the perfect: suddenly do they shoot at him, and fear not.

5 They encourage themselves in an evil matter: they commune of laying snares privily; they say, Who shall see them?

6 They search out iniquities; they accomplish a diligent search: both the inward thought of every one of them, and the heart, is deep.

7 But God shall shoot at them with an

arrow; suddenly shall they be wounded.

8 So they shall make their own tongue to fall upon themselves: all that see them shall flee away.

9 And all men shall fear, and shall declare the work of God; for they shall wisely consider of his doing.

10 The righteous shall be glad in the LORD, and shall trust in him; and all the upright in heart shall glory.

[To the chief Musician, A Psalm and Song of David.]

65:1 Praise waits for you, O God, in Zion: and to you shall the vow be performed.

2 O you that hear prayer, to you shall all flesh come.

3 Iniquities prevail against me: as for our transgressions, you shall purge them away.

4 Blessed is the man whom you choose, and cause to approach to you, that he may dwell in your courts: we shall be satisfied with the goodness of your house, even of your holy temple.

5 By terrible things in righteousness will you answer us, O God of our salvation; who are the confidence of all the ends of the earth, and of them that are afar off upon the sea:

6 Which by his strength sets fast the mountains; being girded with power:

7 Which stills the noise of the seas, the noise of their waves, and the tumult of the people.

8 They also that dwell in the uttermost parts are afraid at your tokens: you make the outgoings of the morning and evening to rejoice.

9 You visit the earth, and water it: you greatly enrich it with the river of God, which is full of water: you prepare them corn, when you have so provided for it.

10 You water the ridges thereof abundantly: you settle the furrows thereof: you make it soft with showers: you bless the springing thereof.

11 You crown the year with your goodness; and your paths drop fatness.

12 They drop upon the pastures of the wilderness: and the little hills rejoice on every side.

13 The pastures are clothed with flocks; the valleys also are covered over with corn; they shout for joy, they also sing.

[To the chief Musician, A Song or Psalm.]

66:1 Make a joyful noise to God, all you[p] lands:

2 Sing forth the honor of his name:

make his praise glorious.

3 Say to God, How terrible are you in your works! through the greatness of your power shall your enemies submit themselves to you.

4 All the earth shall worship you, and shall sing to you; they shall sing to your name. Selah.

5 Come and see the works of God: he is terrible in his doing toward the children of men.

6 He turned the sea into dry land:
they went through the flood on foot:
there did we rejoice in him.

7 He rules by his power for ever; his eyes behold the nations: let not the rebellious exalt themselves. Selah.

8 O bless our God, you[p] people, and make the voice of his praise to be heard:

9 Which holds our soul in life, and suffers not our feet to be moved.

10 For you, O God, have proved us:
you have tried us, as silver is tried.

11 You brought us into the net; you laid affliction upon our loins.

12 You have caused men to ride over our heads; we went through fire and through water: but you brought us out into a wealthy place.

13 I will go into your house with burnt

offerings: I will pay you my vows,

14 Which my lips have uttered, and my mouth has spoken, when I was in trouble.

15 I will offer to you burnt sacrifices of fatlings, with the incense of rams; I will offer bullocks with goats. Selah.

16 Come and hear, all you[p] that fear God, and I will declare what he has done for my soul.

17 I cried to him with my mouth, and he was extolled with my tongue.

18 If I regard iniquity in my heart, the Lord will not hear me:

19 But verily God has heard me; he has attended to the voice of my prayer.

20 Blessed be God, which has not turned away my prayer, nor his mercy from me.

[To the chief Musician on Neginoth, A Psalm or Song.]

67:1 God be merciful to us, and bless us; and cause his face to shine upon us; Selah.

2 That your way may be known upon earth, your saving health among all nations.

3 Let the people praise you, O God; let all the people praise you.

4 O let the nations be glad and sing for joy: for you shall judge the people righteously, and govern the nations upon earth. Selah.

5 Let the people praise you, O God;
let all the people praise you.

6 Then shall the earth yield her increase;
and God, even our own God, shall bless us.

7 God shall bless us; and all the ends
of the earth shall fear him.

[To the chief Musician, A Psalm or Song of David.]

68 :1 Let God arise, let his enemies
be scattered: let them also
that hate him flee before him.

2 As smoke is driven away, so drive them
away: as wax melts before the fire, so let
the wicked perish at the presence of God.

3 But let the righteous be glad; let them rejoice
before God: yes, let them exceedingly rejoice.

4 Sing to God, sing praises to his name:
extol him that rides upon the heavens by
his name YAH, and rejoice before him.

5 A father of the fatherless, and a judge of
the widows, is God in his holy habitation.

6 God sets the solitary in families: he brings
out those which are bound with chains:
but the rebellious dwell in a dry land.

7 O God, when you went forth before
your people, when you did march

through the wilderness; Selah:

8 The earth shook, the heavens also dropped at the presence of God: even Sinai itself was moved at the presence of God, the God of Israel.

9 You, O God, did send a plentiful rain, whereby you did confirm your inheritance, when it was weary.

10 Your congregation has dwelt therein: you, O God, have prepared of your goodness for the poor.

11 The Lord gave the word: great was the company of those that published it.

12 Kings of armies did flee apace: and she that tarried at home divided the spoil.

13 Though you[P] have lien among the pots, yet shall you[P] be as the wings of a dove covered with silver, and her feathers with yellow gold.

14 When the Almighty scattered kings in it, it was white as snow in Salmon.

15 The hill of God is as the hill of Bashan; a high hill as the hill of Bashan.

16 Why leap you[P], you[P] high hills? this is the hill which God desires to dwell in; yes, the LORD will dwell in it for ever.

17 The chariots of God are twenty thousand,

even thousands of angels: the Lord is among them, as in Sinai, in the holy place.

18 You have ascended on high, you have led captivity captive: you have received gifts for men; yes, for the rebellious also, that the LORD God might dwell among them.

19 Blessed be the Lord, who daily loads us with benefits, even the God of our salvation. Selah.

20 He that is our God is the God of salvation; and to God the Lord belong the issues from death.

21 But God shall wound the head of his enemies, and the hairy scalp of such a one as goes on still in his trespasses.

22 The Lord said, I will bring again from Bashan, *I will bring my people again from the depths of the sea:*

23 *That your foot may be dipped in the blood of your enemies, and the tongue of your dogs in the same.*

24 They have seen your goings, O God; even the goings of my God, my King, in the sanctuary.

25 The singers went before, the players on instruments followed after; among them were the damsels playing with timbrels.

26 Bless you^P God in the congregations, even the Lord, from the fountain of Israel.

27 There is little Benjamin with their ruler, the princes of Judah and their council, the princes of Zebulun, and the princes of Naphtali.

28 Your God has commanded your strength: strengthen, O God, that which you have wrought for us.

29 Because of your temple at Jerusalem shall kings bring presents to you.

30 Rebuke the company of spearmen, the multitude of the bulls, with the calves of the people, till every one submit himself with pieces of silver: scatter you the people that delight in war.

31 Princes shall come out of Egypt; Ethiopia shall soon stretch out her hands to God.

32 Sing to God, you[P] kingdoms of the earth; O sing praises to the Lord; Selah:

33 To him that rides upon the heavens of heavens, which were of old; lo, he does send out his voice, and that a mighty voice.

34 Ascribe you[P] strength to God: his excellency is over Israel, and his strength is in the clouds.

35 O God, you are terrible out of your holy places: the God of Israel is he that gives strength and power to his people. Blessed be God.

[To the chief Musician upon Shoshannim, A Psalm of David.]

69:1 Save me, O God; for the waters are come in to my soul.

2 I sink in deep mire, where there is no standing: I am come into deep waters, where the floods overflow me.

3 I am weary of my crying: my throat is dried: my eyes fail while I wait for my God.

4 They that hate me without a cause are more than the hairs of my head: they that would destroy me, being my enemies wrongfully, are mighty: then I restored that which I took not away.

5 O God, you know my foolishness; and my sins are not hid from you.

6 Let not them that wait on you, O Lord God of hosts, be ashamed for my sake: let not those that seek you be confounded for my sake, O God of Israel.

7 Because for your sake I have borne reproach; shame has covered my face.

8 I am become a stranger to my brethren, and an alien to my mother's children.

9 For the zeal of your house has eaten me up; and the reproaches of them that reproached you are fallen upon me.

10 When I wept, and chastened my soul with fasting, that was to my reproach.

11 I made sackcloth also my garment; and I became a proverb to them.

12 They that sit in the gate speak against me; and I was the song of the drunkards.

13 But as for me, my prayer is to you, O LORD, in an acceptable time: O God, in the multitude of your mercy hear me, in the truth of your salvation.

14 Deliver me out of the mire, and let me not sink: let me be delivered from them that hate me, and out of the deep waters.

15 Let not the waterflood overflow me, neither let the deep swallow me up, and let not the pit shut her mouth upon me.

16 Hear me, O LORD; for your lovingkindness is good: turn to me according to the multitude of your tender mercies.

17 And hide not your face from your servant; for I am in trouble: hear me speedily.

18 Draw nigh to my soul, and redeem it: deliver me because of my enemies.

19 You have known my reproach, and my shame, and my dishonor: my adversaries are all before you.

20 Reproach has broken my heart; and I am full of heaviness: and I looked for some to take pity, but there was none; and for comforters, but I found none.

21 They gave me also gall for my meat; and in my thirst they gave me vinegar to drink.

22 Let their table become a snare before them: and that which should have been for their welfare, let it become a trap.

23 Let their eyes be darkened, that they see not; and make their loins continually to shake.

24 Pour out your indignation upon them, and let your wrathful anger take hold of them.

25 Let their habitation be desolate; and let none dwell in their tents.

26 For they persecute him whom you have smitten; and they talk to the grief of those whom you have wounded.

27 Add iniquity to their iniquity: and let them not come into your righteousness.

28 Let them be blotted out of the book of the living, and not be written with the righteous.

29 But I am poor and sorrowful: let your salvation, O God, set me up on high.

30 I will praise the name of God with a song, and will magnify him with thanksgiving.

31 This also shall please the LORD better than an ox or bullock that has horns and hoofs.

32 The humble shall see this, and be glad: and your‎ᵖ heart shall live that seek God.

33 For the LORD hears the poor, and despises not his prisoners.

34 Let the heaven and earth praise him, the seas, and every thing that moves therein.

35 For God will save Zion, and will build the cities of Judah: that they may dwell there, and have it in possession.

36 The seed also of his servants shall inherit it: and they that love his name shall dwell therein.

[To the chief Musician, A Psalm of David, to bring to remembrance.]

70 :1 Make haste, O God, to deliver me; make haste to help me, O LORD.

2 Let them be ashamed and confounded that seek after my soul: let them be turned backward, and put to confusion, that desire my hurt.

3 Let them be turned back for a reward of their shame that say, Aha, aha.

4 Let all those that seek you rejoice and be glad in you: and let such as love your salvation say continually, Let God be magnified.

5 But I am poor and needy: make haste to me, O God: you are my help and my deliverer; O LORD, make no tarrying.

71 :1 In you, O LORD, do I put my trust: let me never be put to confusion.

2 Deliver me in your righteousness, and cause me to escape: incline your ear to me, and save me.

3 Be you my strong habitation, whereunto I may continually resort: you have given commandment to save me; for you are my rock and my fortress.

4 Deliver me, O my God, out of the hand of the wicked, out of the hand of the unrighteous and cruel man.

5 For you are my hope, O Lord God: you are my trust from my youth.

6 By you have I been holden up from the womb: you are he that took me out of my mother's bowels: my praise shall be continually of you.

7 I am as a wonder to many; but you are my strong refuge.

8 Let my mouth be filled with your praise and with your honor all the day.

9 Cast me not off in the time of old age; forsake me not when my strength fails.

10 For my enemies speak against me; and they that lay wait for my soul take counsel together,

11 Saying, God has forsaken him: persecute and take him; for there is none to deliver him.

12 O God, be not far from me: O my God, make haste for my help.

13 Let them be confounded and consumed that are adversaries to my soul; let them be covered with reproach and dishonor that seek my hurt.

14 But I will hope continually, and will yet praise you more and more.

15 My mouth shall show forth your righteousness and your salvation all the day; for I know not the numbers thereof.

16 I will go in the strength of the Lord God: I will make mention of your righteousness, even of you only.

17 O God, you have taught me from my youth: and hitherto have I declared your wondrous works.

18 Now also when I am old and greyheaded, O God, forsake me not; until I have showed your strength to this generation, and your power to every one that is to come.

19 Your righteousness also, O God, is very high, who have done great things: O God, who is like to you!

20 You, which have showed me great and sore troubles, shall quicken me again, and shall bring me up again from the depths of the earth.

21 You shall increase my greatness, and comfort me on every side.

22 I will also praise you with the psaltery, even your truth, O my God: to you will I sing with the harp, O you Holy One of Israel.

23 My lips shall greatly rejoice when I sing to you; and my soul, which you have redeemed.

24 My tongue also shall talk of your righteousness all the day long: for they are confounded, for they are brought to shame, that seek my hurt.

[A Psalm for Solomon.]

72:1 Give the king your judgments, O God, and your righteousness to the king's son.

2 He shall judge your people with righteousness, and your poor with judgment.

3 The mountains shall bring peace to the people, and the little hills, by righteousness.

4 He shall judge the poor of the people, he shall save the children of the needy, and shall break in pieces the oppressor.

5 They shall fear you as long as the sun and moon endure, throughout all generations.

6 He shall come down like rain upon the mown grass: as showers that water the earth.

7 In his days shall the righteous flourish; and abundance of peace so long as the moon endures.

8 He shall have dominion also from sea to sea, and from the river to the ends of the earth.

9 They that dwell in the wilderness shall bow before him; and his enemies shall lick the dust.

10 The kings of Tarshish and of the isles shall bring presents: the kings of Sheba and Seba shall offer gifts.

11 Yes, all kings shall fall down before him: all nations shall serve him.

12 For he shall deliver the needy when he cries; the poor also, and him that has no helper.

13 He shall spare the poor and needy, and shall save the souls of the needy.

14 He shall redeem their soul from deceit and violence: and precious shall their blood be in his sight.

15 And he shall live, and to him shall be given of the gold of Sheba: prayer also shall be made for him continually; and daily shall he be praised.

16 There shall be a handful of corn in the earth upon the top of the mountains; the fruit thereof shall shake like Lebanon: and they of the city shall flourish like grass of the earth.

17 His name shall endure for ever: his name shall be continued as long as the sun: and men shall be blessed in him: all nations shall call him blessed.

18 Blessed be the LORD God, the God of Israel, who only does wondrous things.

19 And blessed be his glorious name for ever: and let the whole earth be filled with his glory; Amen, and Amen.

20 The prayers of David the son of Jesse are ended.

[A Psalm of Asaph.]

73:1 Truly God is good to Israel, even to such as are of a clean heart.

2 But as for me, my feet were almost gone; my steps had well near slipped.

3 For I was envious at the foolish, when I saw the prosperity of the wicked.

4 For there are no bands in their death: but their strength is firm.

5 They are not in trouble as other men; neither are they plagued like other men.

6 Therefore pride compasses them about as a chain; violence covers them as a garment.

7 Their eyes stand out with fatness: they have more than heart could wish.

8 They are corrupt, and speak wickedly concerning oppression: they speak loftily.

9 They set their mouth against the heavens, and their tongue walks through the earth.

10 Therefore his people return here: and waters of a full cup are wrung out to them.

11 And they say, How does God know? and is there knowledge in the most High?

12 Behold, these are the ungodly, who prosper in the world; they increase in riches.

13 Verily I have cleansed my heart in vain, and washed my hands in innocency.

14 For all the day long have I been plagued, and chastened every morning.

15 If I say, I will speak thus; behold, I should offend against the generation of your children.

16 When I thought to know this, it was too painful for me;

17 Until I went into the sanctuary of God; then understood I their end.

18 Surely you did set them in slippery places: you cast them down into destruction.

19 How are they brought into desolation, as in a moment! they are utterly consumed with terrors.

20 As a dream when one awakes; so, O Lord, when you awake, you shall despise their image.

21 Thus my heart was grieved, and I was pricked in my reins.

22 So foolish was I, and ignorant: I was as a beast before you.

23 Nevertheless I am continually with you: you have held me by my right hand.

24 You shall guide me with your counsel, and afterward receive me to glory.

25 Whom have I in heaven but you? and there is none upon earth that I desire beside you.

26 My flesh and my heart fails: but God is the strength of my heart, and my portion for ever.

27 For, lo, they that are far from you shall perish: you have destroyed all them that go a whoring from you.

28 But it is good for me to draw near to God: I have put my trust in the Lord God, that I may declare all your works.

[Maschil of Asaph.]

74:1 O God, why have you cast us off for ever? why does your anger smoke against the sheep of your pasture?

2 Remember your congregation, which

you have purchased of old; the rod of your inheritance, which you have redeemed; this mount Zion, wherein you have dwelt.

3 Lift up your feet to the perpetual desolations; even all that the enemy has done wickedly in the sanctuary.

4 Your enemies roar in the midst of your congregations; they set up their ensigns for signs.

5 A man was famous according as he had lifted up axes upon the thick trees.

6 But now they break down the carved work thereof at once with axes and hammers.

7 They have cast fire into your sanctuary, they have defiled by casting down the dwelling place of your name to the ground.

8 They said in their hearts, Let us destroy them together: they have burned up all the synagogues of God in the land.

9 We see not our signs: there is no more any prophet: neither is there among us any that knows how long.

10 O God, how long shall the adversary reproach? shall the enemy blaspheme your name for ever?

11 Why withdraw you your hand, even your right hand? pluck it out of your bosom.

12 For God is my King of old, working salvation in the midst of the earth.

13 You did divide the sea by your strength: you broke the heads of the dragons in the waters.

14 You broke the heads of leviathan in pieces, and gave him to be meat to the people inhabiting the wilderness.

15 You did cleave the fountain and the flood: you dried up mighty rivers.

16 The day is yours, the night also is yours: you have prepared the light and the sun.

17 You have set all the borders of the earth: you have made summer and winter.

18 Remember this, that the enemy has reproached, O LORD, and that the foolish people have blasphemed your name.

19 O deliver not the soul of your turtledove to the multitude of the wicked: forget not the congregation of your poor for ever.

20 Have respect to the covenant: for the dark places of the earth are full of the habitations of cruelty.

21 O let not the oppressed return ashamed: let the poor and needy praise your name.

22 Arise, O God, plead your own cause: remember how the foolish man reproaches you daily.

23 Forget not the voice of your enemies:
the tumult of those that rise up
against you increases continually.

[To the chief Musician, Altaschith,
A Psalm or Song of Asaph.]

75 :1 Unto you, O God, do we give thanks,
to you do we give thanks: for that your
name is near your wondrous works declare.

2 *When I shall receive the congregation*
I will judge uprightly.

3 *The earth and all the inhabitants thereof are*
dissolved: I bear up the pillars of it. Selah.

4 *I said to the fools, Deal not foolishly:*
and to the wicked, Lift not up the horn:

5 *Lift not up your[p] horn on high:*
speak not with a stiff neck.

6 For promotion comes neither from the east,
nor from the west, nor from the south.

7 But God is the judge: he puts
down one, and sets up another.

8 For in the hand of the LORD there is a
cup, and the wine is red; it is full of mixture;
and he pours out of the same: but the
dregs thereof, all the wicked of the earth
shall wring them out, and drink them.

9 But I will declare for ever; I will
sing praises to the God of Jacob.

10 _All the horns of the wicked also will I cut off;_
but the horns of the righteous shall be exalted.

[To the chief Musician on Neginoth,
A Psalm or Song of Asaph.]

76:1 In Judah is God known: his
name is great in Israel.

2 In Salem also is his tabernacle,
and his dwelling place in Zion.

3 There brake he the arrows of the bow, the
shield, and the sword, and the battle. Selah.

4 You are more glorious and excellent
than the mountains of prey.

5 The stouthearted are spoiled, they
have slept their sleep: and none of the
men of might have found their hands.

6 At your rebuke, O God of Jacob, both the
chariot and horse are cast into a dead sleep.

7 You, even you, are to be feared: and who may
stand in your sight when once you are angry?

8 You did cause judgment to be heard from
heaven; the earth feared, and was still,

9 When God arose to judgment, to save
all the meek of the earth. Selah.

10 Surely the wrath of man shall praise you:

the remainder of wrath shall you restrain.

11 Vow, and pay to the LORD your God:
let all that be round about him bring
presents to him that ought to be feared.

12 He shall cut off the spirit of princes:
he is terrible to the kings of the earth.

[To the chief Musician, to Jeduthun,
A Psalm of Asaph.]

77:1 I cried to God with my
voice, even to God with my
voice; and he gave ear to me.

2 In the day of my trouble I sought the
Lord: my sore ran in the night, and ceased
not: my soul refused to be comforted.

3 I remembered God, and was
troubled: I complained, and my
spirit was overwhelmed. Selah.

4 You hold my eyes waking: I am so
troubled that I cannot speak.

5 I have considered the days of old,
the years of ancient times.

6 I call to remembrance my song in the
night: I commune with my own heart:
and my spirit made diligent search.

7 Will the Lord cast off for ever? and
will he be favorable no more?

8 Is his mercy clean gone for ever?
does his promise fail for evermore?

9 Has God forgotten to be gracious? has he
in anger shut up his tender mercies? Selah.

10 And I said, This is my infirmity:
but I will remember the years of the
right hand of the most High.

11 I will remember the works of the LORD:
surely I will remember your wonders of old.

12 I will meditate also of all your
work, and talk of your doings.

13 Your way, O God, is in the sanctuary:
who is so great a God as our God?

14 You are the God that does wonders: you
have declared your strength among the people.

15 You have with your arm redeemed your
people, the sons of Jacob and Joseph. Selah.

16 The waters saw you, O God, the
waters saw you; they were afraid:
the depths also were troubled.

17 The clouds poured out water: the skies sent
out a sound: your arrows also went abroad.

18 The voice of your thunder was in the
heaven: the lightnings lightened the
world: the earth trembled and shook.

19 Your way is in the sea, and your path in the

great waters, and your footsteps are not known.
20 You led your people like a flock by the hand of Moses and Aaron.

[Maschil of Asaph.]

78 :1 Give ear, O my people, to my law: incline your ears to the words of my mouth.

2 I will open my mouth in a parable: I will utter dark sayings of old:

3 Which we have heard and known, and our fathers have told us.

4 We will not hide them from their children, showing to the generation to come the praises of the LORD, and his strength, and his wonderful works that he has done.

5 For he established a testimony in Jacob, and appointed a law in Israel, which he commanded our fathers, that they should make them known to their children:

6 That the generation to come might know them, even the children which should be born; who should arise and declare them to their children:

7 That they might set their hope in God, and not forget the works of God, but keep his commandments:

8 And might not be as their fathers, a stubborn and rebellious generation; a generation that set not their heart aright, and whose spirit was not steadfast with God.

9 The children of Ephraim, being armed, and carrying bows, turned back in the day of battle.

10 They kept not the covenant of God, and refused to walk in his law;

11 And forgot his works, and his wonders that he had showed them.

12 Marvellous things did he in the sight of their fathers, in the land of Egypt, in the field of Zoan.

13 He divided the sea, and caused them to pass through; and he made the waters to stand as a heap.

14 In the daytime also he led them with a cloud, and all the night with a light of fire.

15 He clave the rocks in the wilderness, and gave them drink as out of the great depths.

16 He brought streams also out of the rock, and caused waters to run down like rivers.

17 And they sinned yet more against him by provoking the most High in the wilderness.

18 And they tempted God in their heart by asking meat for their lust.

19 Yes, they spoke against God; they said,

PSALM 78

Can God furnish a table in the wilderness?

20 Behold, he smote the rock, that the waters gushed out, and the streams overflowed; can he give bread also? can he provide flesh for his people?

21 Therefore the LORD heard this, and was wroth: so a fire was kindled against Jacob, and anger also came up against Israel;

22 Because they believed not in God, and trusted not in his salvation:

23 Though he had commanded the clouds from above, and opened the doors of heaven,

24 And had rained down manna upon them to eat, and had given them of the corn of heaven.

25 Man did eat angels' food: he sent them meat to the full.

26 He caused an east wind to blow in the heaven: and by his power he brought in the south wind.

27 He rained flesh also upon them as dust, and feathered fowls like as the sand of the sea:

28 And he let it fall in the midst of their camp, round about their habitations.

29 So they did eat, and were well filled: for he gave them their own desire;

30 They were not estranged from their lust.

But while their meat was yet in their mouths,

31 The wrath of God came upon them, and slew the fattest of them, and smote down the chosen men of Israel.

32 For all this they sinned still, and believed not for his wondrous works.

33 Therefore their days did he consume in vanity, and their years in trouble.

34 When he slew them, then they sought him: and they returned and inquired early after God.

35 And they remembered that God was their rock, and the high God their redeemer.

36 Nevertheless they did flatter him with their mouth, and they lied to him with their tongues.

37 For their heart was not right with him, neither were they steadfast in his covenant.

38 But he, being full of compassion, forgave their iniquity, and destroyed them not: yes, many a time turned he his anger away, and did not stir up all his wrath.

39 For he remembered that they were but flesh; a wind that passes away, and comes not again.

40 How oft did they provoke him in the wilderness, and grieve him in the desert!

41 Yes, they turned back and tempted God, and limited the Holy One of Israel.

42 They remembered not his hand, nor the day when he delivered them from the enemy.

43 How he had wrought his signs in Egypt, and his wonders in the field of Zoan.

44 And had turned their rivers into blood; and their floods, that they could not drink.

45 He sent divers sorts of flies among them, which devoured them; and frogs, which destroyed them.

46 He gave also their increase to the caterpiller, and their labor to the locust.

47 He destroyed their vines with hail, and their sycomore trees with frost.

48 He gave up their cattle also to the hail, and their flocks to hot thunderbolts.

49 He cast upon them the fierceness of his anger, wrath, and indignation, and trouble, by sending evil angels among them.

50 He made a way to his anger; he spared not their soul from death, but gave their life over to the pestilence;

51 And smote all the firstborn in Egypt; the chief of their strength in the tabernacles of Ham:

52 But made his own people to go forth like sheep, and guided them in the wilderness like a flock.

53 And he led them on safely, so that they feared not: but the sea overwhelmed their enemies.

54 And he brought them to the border of his sanctuary, even to this mountain, which his right hand had purchased.

55 He cast out the heathen also before them, and divided them an inheritance by line, and made the tribes of Israel to dwell in their tents.

56 Yet they tempted and provoked the most high God, and kept not his testimonies:

57 But turned back, and dealt unfaithfully like their fathers: they were turned aside like a deceitful bow.

58 For they provoked him to anger with their high places, and moved him to jealousy with their graven images.

59 When God heard this, he was wroth, and greatly abhorred Israel:

60 So that he forsook the tabernacle of Shiloh, the tent which he placed among men;

61 And delivered his strength into captivity, and his glory into the enemy's hand.

62 He gave his people over also to the sword; and was wroth with his inheritance.

63 The fire consumed their young men; and

their maidens were not given to marriage.

64 Their priests fell by the sword; and their widows made no lamentation.

65 Then the Lord awaked as one out of sleep, and like a mighty man that shouts by reason of wine.

66 And he smote his enemies in the hinder parts: he put them to a perpetual reproach.

67 Moreover he refused the tabernacle of Joseph, and chose not the tribe of Ephraim:

68 But chose the tribe of Judah, the mount Zion which he loved.

69 And he built his sanctuary like high palaces, like the earth which he has established for ever.

70 He chose David also his servant, and took him from the sheepfolds:

71 From following the ewes great with young he brought him to feed Jacob his people, and Israel his inheritance.

72 So he fed them according to the integrity of his heart; and guided them by the skillfulness of his hands.

[A Psalm of Asaph.]

79:1 O God, the heathen are come into your inheritance; your holy temple have they defiled; they have laid Jerusalem on heaps.

2 The dead bodies of your servants have they given to be meat to the fowls of the heaven, the flesh of your saints to the beasts of the earth.

3 Their blood have they shed like water round about Jerusalem; and there was none to bury them.

4 We are become a reproach to our neighbors, a scorn and derision to them that are round about us.

5 How long, LORD? will you be angry for ever? shall your jealousy burn like fire?

6 Pour out your wrath upon the heathen that have not known you, and upon the kingdoms that have not called upon your name.

7 For they have devoured Jacob, and laid waste his dwelling place.

8 O remember not against us former iniquities: let your tender mercies speedily prevent us: for we are brought very low.

9 Help us, O God of our salvation, for the glory of your name: and deliver us, and purge away our sins, for your name's sake.

10 Wherefore should the heathen say, Where is their God? let him be known among the heathen in our sight by the revenging of the blood of your servants which is shed.

11 Let the sighing of the prisoner come before

you; according to the greatness of your power preserve you those that are appointed to die;

12 And render to our neighbors sevenfold into their bosom their reproach, wherewith they have reproached you, O Lord.

13 So we your people and sheep of your pasture will give you thanks for ever: we will show forth your praise to all generations.

[To the chief Musician upon Shoshannimeduth, A Psalm of Asaph.]

80:1 Give ear, O Shepherd of Israel, you that lead Joseph like a flock; you that dwell between the cherubims, shine forth.

2 Before Ephraim and Benjamin and Manasseh stir up your strength, and come and save us.

3 Turn us again, O God, and cause your face to shine; and we shall be saved.

4 O LORD God of hosts, how long will you be angry against the prayer of your people?

5 You feed them with the bread of tears; and give them tears to drink in great measure.

6 You make us a strife to our neighbors: and our enemies laugh among themselves.

7 Turn us again, O God of hosts, and cause your face to shine; and we shall be saved.

8 You have brought a vine out of Egypt: you

have cast out the heathen, and planted it.

9 You prepared room before it, and did cause it to take deep root, and it filled the land.

10 The hills were covered with the shadow of it, and the boughs thereof were like the goodly cedars.

11 She sent out her boughs to the sea, and her branches to the river.

12 Why have you then broken down her hedges, so that all they which pass by the way do pluck her?

13 The boar out of the wood does waste it, and the wild beast of the field does devour it.

14 Return, we beseech you, O God of hosts: look down from heaven, and behold, and visit this vine;

15 And the vineyard which your right hand has planted, and the branch that you made strong for yourself.

16 It is burned with fire, it is cut down: they perish at the rebuke of your countenance.

17 Let your hand be upon the man of your right hand, upon the son of man whom you made strong for yourself.

18 So will not we go back from you: quicken us, and we will call upon your name.

19 Turn us again, O LORD God of hosts, cause your face to shine; and we shall be saved.

[To the chief Musician upon Gittith, A Psalm of Asaph.]

81 **:1** Sing aloud to God our strength: make a joyful noise to the God of Jacob.

2 Take a psalm, and bring here the timbrel, the pleasant harp with the psaltery.

3 Blow up the trumpet in the new moon, in the time appointed, on our solemn feast day.

4 For this was a statute for Israel, and a law of the God of Jacob.

5 This he ordained in Joseph for a testimony, when he went out through the land of Egypt: where I heard a language that I understood not.

6 *I removed his shoulder from the burden: his hands were delivered from the pots.*

7 *You called in trouble, and I delivered you; I answered you in the secret place of thunder: I proved you at the waters of Meribah.* Selah.

8 *Hear, O my people, and I will testify to you: O Israel, if you will hearken to me;*

9 *There shall no strange god be in you; neither shall you worship any strange god.*

10 *I am the LORD your God, which brought you out of the land of Egypt:*

open your mouth wide, and I will fill it.

11 *But my people would not hearken to my voice; and Israel would none of me.*

12 *So I gave them up to their own hearts' lust: and they walked in their own counsels.*

13 *Oh that my people had hearkened to me, and Israel had walked in my ways!*

14 *I should soon have subdued their enemies, and turned my hand against their adversaries.*

15 *The haters of the LORD should have submitted themselves to him: but their time should have endured for ever.*

16 *He should have fed them also with the finest of the wheat: and with honey out of the rock should I have satisfied you.*

[A Psalm of Asaph.]

82 **:1** God stands in the congregation of the mighty; he judges among the gods.
2 *How long will you*ᵖ *judge unjustly, and accept the persons of the wicked?* Selah.

3 *Defend the poor and fatherless: do justice to the afflicted and needy.*

4 *Deliver the poor and needy: rid them out of the hand of the wicked.*

5 *They know not, neither will they understand; they walk on in darkness: all the* *foundations of the earth are out of course.*

6 *I have said, You^P are gods; and all of you^P are children of the most High.*

7 *But you^P shall die like men, and fall like one of the princes.*

8 Arise, O God, judge the earth: for you shall inherit all nations.

[A Song or Psalm of Asaph.]

83:1 Keep not you silence, O God: hold not your peace, and be not still, O God.

2 For, lo, your enemies make a tumult: and they that hate you have lifted up the head.

3 They have taken crafty counsel against your people, and consulted against your hidden ones.

4 They have said, Come, and let us cut them off from being a nation; that the name of Israel may be no more in remembrance

5 For they have consulted together with one consent: they are confederate against you:

6 The tabernacles of Edom, and the Ishmaelites; of Moab, and the Hagarenes;

7 Gebal, and Ammon, and Amalek; the Philistines with the inhabitants of Tyre;

8 Assur also is joined with them: they have helped the children of Lot. Selah.

9 Do to them as to the Midianites; as to

Sisera, as to Jabin, at the brook of Kison:

10 Which perished at Endor: they became as dung for the earth.

11 Make their nobles like Oreb, and like Zeeb: yes, all their princes as Zebah, and as Zalmunna:

12 Who said, Let us take to ourselves the houses of God in possession.

13 O my God, make them like a wheel; as the stubble before the wind.

14 As the fire burns a wood, and as the flame sets the mountains on fire;

15 So persecute them with your tempest, and make them afraid with your storm.

16 Fill their faces with shame; that they may seek your name, O LORD.

17 Let them be confounded and troubled for ever; yes, let them be put to shame, and perish:

18 That men may know that you, whose name alone is YEHOVAH, are the most high over all the earth.

[To the chief Musician upon Gittith, A Psalm for the sons of Korah.]

84 :1 How amiable are your tabernacles, O LORD of hosts!

PSALM 84

2 My soul longs, yes, even faints for the courts of the LORD: my heart and my flesh cries out for the living God.

3 Yes, the sparrow has found a house, and the swallow a nest for herself, where she may lay her young, even your altars, O LORD of hosts, my King, and my God.

4 Blessed are they that dwell in your house: they will be still praising you. Selah.

5 Blessed is the man whose strength is in you; in whose heart are the ways of them.

6 Who passing through the valley of Baca make it a well; the rain also fills the pools.

7 They go from strength to strength, every one of them in Zion appears before God.

8 O LORD God of hosts, hear my prayer: give ear, O God of Jacob. Selah.

9 Behold, O God our shield, and look upon the face of your anointed.

10 For a day in your courts is better than a thousand. I had rather be a doorkeeper in the house of my God, than to dwell in the tents of wickedness.

11 For the LORD God is a sun and shield: the LORD will give grace and glory: no good thing will he withhold from them that walk uprightly.

Books of the Bible—Psalms

12 O LORD of hosts, blessed is
the man that trusts in you.

[To the chief Musician, A Psalm
for the sons of Korah.]

85 :1 LORD, you have been favorable
to your land: you have brought
back the captivity of Jacob.

2 You have forgiven the iniquity of your
people, you have covered all their sin. Selah.

3 You have taken away all your
wrath: you have turned yourself from
the fierceness of your anger.

4 Turn us, O God of our salvation, and
cause your anger toward us to cease.

5 Will you be angry with us for ever? will you
draw out your anger to all generations?

6 Will you not revive us again: that
your people may rejoice in you?

7 Show us your mercy, O LORD,
and grant us your salvation.

8 I will hear what God the LORD will speak: for
he will speak peace to his people, and to his
saints: but let them not turn again to folly.

9 Surely his salvation is near them that fear
him; that glory may dwell in our land.

10 Mercy and truth are met together;

righteousness and peace have kissed each other.

11 Truth shall spring out of the earth; and righteousness shall look down from heaven.

12 Yes, the LORD shall give that which is good; and our land shall yield her increase.

13 Righteousness shall go before him; and shall set us in the way of his steps.

[A Prayer of David.]

86 **:1** Bow down your ear, O LORD, hear me: for I am poor and needy.

2 Preserve my soul; for I am holy: O you my God, save your servant that trusts in you.

3 Be merciful to me, O Lord: for I cry to you daily.

4 Rejoice the soul of your servant: for to you, O Lord, do I lift up my soul.

5 For you, Lord, are good, and ready to forgive; and plenteous in mercy to all them that call upon you.

6 Give ear, O LORD, to my prayer; and attend to the voice of my supplications.

7 In the day of my trouble I will call upon you: for you will answer me.

8 Among the gods there is none like to you, O Lord; neither are there any works like to your works.

9 All nations whom you have made
shall come and worship before you, O
Lord; and shall glorify your name.

10 For you are great, and do wondrous
things: you are God alone.

11 Teach me your way, O LORD; I will walk in
your truth: unite my heart to fear your name.

12 I will praise you, O Lord my God, with all my
heart: and I will glorify your name for evermore.

13 For great is your mercy toward me: and you
have delivered my soul from the lowest hell.

14 O God, the proud are risen against me, and
the assemblies of violent men have sought after
my soul; and have not set you before them.

15 But you, O Lord, are a God full of
compassion, and gracious, long suffering,
and plenteous in mercy and truth.

16 O turn to me, and have mercy upon
me; give your strength to your servant,
and save the son of your handmaid.

17 Show me a token for good; that they which
hate me may see it, and be ashamed: because
you, LORD, have helped me, and comforted me.

[A Psalm or Song for the sons of Korah.]

87 :1 His foundation is in the holy mountains.
2 The LORD loves the gates of Zion

more than all the dwellings of Jacob.

3 Glorious things are spoken of
you, O city of God. Selah.

4 I will make mention of Rahab and Babylon
to them that know me: behold Philistia, and
Tyre, with Ethiopia; this man was born there.

5 And of Zion it shall be said, This and
that man was born in her: and the
highest himself shall establish her.

6 The LORD shall count, when he writes up the
people, that this man was born there. Selah.

7 As well the singers as the players
on instruments shall be there:
all my springs are in you.

[A Song or Psalm for the sons of Korah, to
the chief Musician upon Mahalath Leannoth,
Maschil of Heman the Ezrahite.]

88 :1 O LORD God of my salvation, I have
cried day and night before you:

2 Let my prayer come before you:
incline your ear to my cry;

3 For my soul is full of troubles: and
my life draws near to the grave.

4 I am counted with them that go down into
the pit: I am as a man that has no strength:

5 Free among the dead, like the slain that

lie in the grave, whom you remember no more: and they are cut off from your hand.

6 You have laid me in the lowest pit, in darkness, in the deeps.

7 Your wrath lies hard upon me, and you have afflicted me with all your waves. Selah.

8 You have put away my acquaintance far from me; you have made me an abomination to them: I am shut up, and I cannot come forth.

9 My eye mourns by reason of affliction: LORD, I have called daily upon you, I have stretched out my hands to you.

10 Will you show wonders to the dead? shall the dead arise and praise you? Selah.

11 Shall your lovingkindness be declared in the grave? or your faithfulness in destruction?

12 Shall your wonders be known in the dark? and your righteousness in the land of forgetfulness?

13 But to you have I cried, O LORD; and in the morning shall my prayer prevent you.

14 LORD, why cast you off my soul? why hide you your face from me?

15 I am afflicted and ready to die from my youth up: while I suffer your terrors I am distracted.

16 Your fierce wrath goes over me;

your terrors have cut me off.

17 They came round about me daily like water; they compassed me about together.

18 Lover and friend have you put far from me, and my acquaintance into darkness.

[Maschil of Ethan the Ezrahite.]

89:1 I will sing of the mercies of the LORD for ever: with my mouth will I make known your faithfulness to all generations.

2 For I have said, Mercy shall be built up for ever: your faithfulness shall you establish in the very heavens.

3 *I have made a covenant with my chosen, I have sworn to David my servant,*

4 *Your seed will I establish for ever, and build up your throne to all generations.* Selah.

5 And the heavens shall praise your wonders, O LORD: your faithfulness also in the congregation of the saints.

6 For who in the heaven can be compared to the LORD? who among the sons of the mighty can be likened to the LORD?

7 God is greatly to be feared in the assembly of the saints, and to be had in reverence of all them that are about him.

8 O LORD God of hosts, who is a

strong LORD like to you? or to your faithfulness round about you?

9 You rule the raging of the sea: when the waves thereof arise, you still them.

10 You have broken Rahab in pieces, as one that is slain; you have scattered your enemies with your strong arm.

11 The heavens are yours, the earth also is yours: as for the world and the fulness thereof, you have founded them.

12 The north and the south you have created them: Tabor and Hermon shall rejoice in your name.

13 You have a mighty arm: strong is your hand, and high is your right hand.

14 Justice and judgment are the habitation of your throne: mercy and truth shall go before your face.

15 Blessed is the people that know the joyful sound: they shall walk, O LORD, in the light of your countenance.

16 In your name shall they rejoice all the day: and in your righteousness shall they be exalted.

17 For you are the glory of their strength: and in your favor our horn shall be exalted.

18 For the LORD is our defense; and

the Holy One of Israel is our king.

19 Then you spoke in vision to your holy one, and said, *I have laid help upon one that is mighty; I have exalted one chosen out of the people.*

20 *I have found David my servant; with my holy oil have I anointed him:*

21 *With whom my hand shall be established: my arm also shall strengthen him.*

22 *The enemy shall not exact upon him; nor the son of wickedness afflict him.*

23 *And I will beat down his foes before his face, and plague them that hate him.*

24 *But my faithfulness and my mercy shall be with him: and in my name shall his horn be exalted.*

25 *I will set his hand also in the sea, and his right hand in the rivers.*

26 *He shall cry to me, You are my father, my God, and the rock of my salvation.*

27 *Also I will make him my firstborn, higher than the kings of the earth.*

28 *My mercy will I keep for him for evermore, and my covenant shall stand fast with him.*

29 *His seed also will I make to endure for ever, and his throne as the days of heaven.*

30 *If his children forsake my law, and walk not in my judgments;*

31 *If they break my statutes, and keep not my commandments;*

32 *Then will I visit their transgression with the rod, and their iniquity with stripes.*

33 *Nevertheless my lovingkindness will I not utterly take from him, nor suffer my faithfulness to fail.*

34 *My covenant will I not break, nor alter the thing that is gone out of my lips.*

35 *Once have I sworn by my holiness that I will not lie to David.*

36 *His seed shall endure for ever, and his throne as the sun before me.*

37 *It shall be established for ever as the moon, and as a faithful witness in heaven.* Selah.

38 But you have cast off and abhorred, you have been wroth with your anointed.

39 You have made void the covenant of your servant: you have profaned his crown by casting it to the ground.

40 You have broken down all his hedges; you have brought his strong holds to ruin.

41 All that pass by the way spoil him: he is a reproach to his neighbors.

42 You have set up the right hand
of his adversaries; you have made
all his enemies to rejoice.

43 You have also turned the edge of his sword,
and have not made him to stand in the battle.

44 You have made his glory to cease, and
cast his throne down to the ground.

45 The days of his youth have you shortened:
you have covered him with shame. Selah.

46 How long, LORD? will you hide yourself
for ever? shall your wrath burn like fire?

47 Remember how short my time is:
wherefore have you made all men in vain?

48 What man is he that lives, and shall
not see death? shall he deliver his soul
from the hand of the grave? Selah.

49 Lord, where are your former
lovingkindnesses, which you swore
to David in your truth?

50 Remember, Lord, the reproach of your
servants; how I do bear in my bosom
the reproach of all the mighty people;

51 Wherewith your enemies have reproached,
O LORD; wherewith they have reproached
the footsteps of your anointed.

52 Blessed be the LORD for evermore.

Amen, and Amen.

[A Prayer of Moses the man of God.]

90:1 Lord, you have been our dwelling place in all generations.

2 Before the mountains were brought forth, or ever you had formed the earth and the world, even from everlasting to everlasting, you are God.

3 You turn man to destruction; and say, _Return, you_ᵖ _children of men._

4 For a thousand years in your sight are but as yesterday when it is past, and as a watch in the night.

5 You carry them away as with a flood; they are as a sleep: in the morning they are like grass which grows up.

6 In the morning it flourishes, and grows up; in the evening it is cut down, and withers.

7 For we are consumed by your anger, and by your wrath are we troubled.

8 You have set our iniquities before you, our secret sins in the light of your countenance.

9 For all our days are passed away in your wrath: we spend our years as a tale that is told.

10 The days of our years are threescore years and ten; and if by reason of strength they be fourscore years, yet is their strength labor and sorrow; for it is soon cut off, and we fly away.

11 Who knows the power of your anger? even according to your fear, so is your wrath.

12 So teach us to number our days, that we may apply our hearts to wisdom.

13 Return, O LORD, how long? and let it repent you concerning your servants.

14 O satisfy us early with your mercy; that we may rejoice and be glad all our days.

15 Make us glad according to the days wherein you have afflicted us, and the years wherein we have seen evil.

16 Let your work appear to your servants, and your glory to their children.

17 And let the beauty of the LORD our God be upon us: and establish you the work of our hands upon us; yes, the work of our hands establish you it.

91:1 He that dwells in the secret place of the most High shall abide under the shadow of the Almighty.

2 I will say of the LORD, He is my refuge and my fortress: my God; in him will I trust.

3 Surely he shall deliver you from the snare of the fowler, and from the noisome pestilence.

4 He shall cover you with his feathers, and under his wings shall you trust: his truth shall be your shield and buckler.

5 You shall not be afraid for the terror by night; nor for the arrow that flies by day;

6 Nor for the pestilence that walks in darkness; nor for the destruction that wastes at noonday.

7 A thousand shall fall at your side, and ten thousand at your right hand; but it shall not come near you.

8 Only with your eyes shall you behold and see the reward of the wicked.

9 Because you have made the LORD, which is my refuge, even the most High, your habitation;

10 There shall no evil befall you, neither shall any plague come near your dwelling.

11 For he shall give his angels charge over you, to keep you in all your ways.

12 They shall bear you up in their hands, lest you dash your foot against a stone.

13 You shall tread upon the lion and adder: the young lion and the dragon shall you trample under feet.

14 *Because he has set his love upon me, therefore will I deliver him: I will set him on high, because he has known my name.*

15 *He shall call upon me, and I will answer him: I will be with him in trouble; I will deliver him, and honor him.*
16 *With long life will I satisfy him, and show him my salvation.*

[A Psalm or Song for the sabbath day.]

92:1 It is a good thing to give thanks to the LORD, and to sing praises to your name, O Most High:
2 To show forth your lovingkindness in the morning, and your faithfulness every night,
3 Upon an instrument of ten strings, and upon the psaltery; upon the harp with a solemn sound.
4 For you, LORD, have made me glad through your work: I will triumph in the works of your hands.
5 O LORD, how great are your works! and your thoughts are very deep.
6 A brutish man knows not; neither does a fool understand this.
7 When the wicked spring as the grass, and when all the workers of iniquity do flourish; it is that they shall be destroyed for ever:
8 But you, LORD, are most high for evermore.
9 For, lo, your enemies, O LORD, for,

lo, your enemies shall perish; all the workers of iniquity shall be scattered.

10 But my horn shall you exalt like the horn of a unicorn: I shall be anointed with fresh oil.

11 My eye also shall see my desire on my enemies, and my ears shall hear my desire of the wicked that rise up against me.

12 The righteous shall flourish like the palm tree: he shall grow like a cedar in Lebanon.

13 Those that be planted in the house of the LORD shall flourish in the courts of our God.

14 They shall still bring forth fruit in old age; they shall be fat and flourishing;

15 To show that the LORD is upright: he is my rock, and there is no unrighteousness in him.

93 :1 The LORD reigns, he is clothed with majesty; the LORD is clothed with strength, wherewith he has girded himself: the world also is established, that it cannot be moved.

2 Your throne is established of old: you are from everlasting.

3 The floods have lifted up, O LORD, the floods have lifted up their voice; the floods lift up their waves.

4 The LORD on high is mightier than

the noise of many waters, yes, than the mighty waves of the sea.

5 Your testimonies are very sure: holiness becomes your house, O LORD, for ever.

94:1 O LORD God, to whom vengeance belongs; O God, to whom vengeance belongs, show yourself.

2 Lift up yourself, you judge of the earth: render a reward to the proud.

3 LORD, how long shall the wicked, how long shall the wicked triumph?

4 How long shall they utter and speak hard things? and all the workers of iniquity boast themselves?

5 They break in pieces your people, O LORD, and afflict your heritage.

6 They slay the widow and the stranger, and murder the fatherless.

7 Yet they say, The LORD shall not see, neither shall the God of Jacob regard it.

8 Understand, you^P brutish among the people: and you^P fools, when will you^P be wise?

9 He that planted the ear, shall he not hear? he that formed the eye, shall he not see?

10 He that chastises the heathen, shall not he correct? he that teaches man knowledge, shall not he know?

11 The LORD knows the thoughts
of man, that they are vanity.

12 Blessed is the man whom you chasten,
O LORD, and teach him out of your law;

13 That you may give him rest from the days of
adversity, until the pit be dug for the wicked.

14 For the LORD will not cast off his people,
neither will he forsake his inheritance.

15 But judgment shall return to righteousness:
and all the upright in heart shall follow it.

16 Who will rise up for me against the
evildoers? or who will stand up for me
against the workers of iniquity?

17 Unless the LORD had been my help,
my soul had almost dwelt in silence.

18 When I said, My foot slips; your
mercy, O LORD, held me up.

19 In the multitude of my thoughts within
me your comforts delight my soul.

20 Shall the throne of iniquity have fellowship
with you, which frames mischief by a law?

21 They gather themselves together
against the soul of the righteous, and
condemn the innocent blood.

22 But the LORD is my defense; and

my God is the rock of my refuge.

23 And he shall bring upon them their own iniquity, and shall cut them off in their own wickedness; yes, the LORD our God shall cut them off.

95:1 O come, let us sing to the LORD: let us make a joyful noise to the rock of our salvation.

2 Let us come before his presence with thanksgiving, and make a joyful noise to him with psalms.

3 For the LORD is a great God, and a great King above all gods.

4 In his hand are the deep places of the earth: the strength of the hills is his also.

5 The sea is his, and he made it: and his hands formed the dry land.

6 O come, let us worship and bow down: let us kneel before the LORD our maker.

7 For he is our God; and we are the people of his pasture, and the sheep of his hand. To day if you^P will hear his voice,

8 *Harden not your^P heart, as in the provocation, and as in the day of temptation in the wilderness:*

9 *When your^P fathers tempted me,*

proved me, and saw my work.

10 *Forty years long was I grieved with this generation, and said, It is a people that do err in their heart, and they have not known my ways:*

11 *To whom I swore in my wrath that they should not enter into my rest.*

96

:1 O sing to the LORD a new song: sing to the LORD, all the earth.

2 Sing to the LORD, bless his name; show forth his salvation from day to day.

3 Declare his glory among the heathen, his wonders among all people.

4 For the LORD is great, and greatly to be praised: he is to be feared above all gods.

5 For all the gods of the nations are idols: but the LORD made the heavens.

6 Honor and majesty are before him: strength and beauty are in his sanctuary.

7 Give to the LORD, O you[p] kindreds of the people, give to the LORD glory and strength.

8 Give to the LORD the glory due to his name: bring an offering, and come into his courts.

9 O worship the LORD in the beauty of holiness: fear before him, all the earth.

10 Say among the heathen that the

LORD reigns: the world also shall be established that it shall not be moved: he shall judge the people righteously.

11 Let the heavens rejoice, and let the earth be glad; let the sea roar, and the fulness thereof.

12 Let the field be joyful, and all that is therein: then shall all the trees of the wood rejoice

13 Before the LORD: for he comes, for he comes to judge the earth: he shall judge the world with righteousness, and the people with his truth.

97 **:1** The LORD reigns; let the earth rejoice; let the multitude of isles be glad thereof.

2 Clouds and darkness are round about him: righteousness and judgment are the habitation of his throne.

3 A fire goes before him, and burns up his enemies round about.

4 His lightnings enlightened the world: the earth saw, and trembled.

5 The hills melted like wax at the presence of the Lord, at the presence of the LORD of the whole earth.

6 The heavens declare his righteousness, and all the people see his glory.

7 Confounded be all they that serve graven images, that boast themselves of idols: worship him, all you[P] gods.

8 Zion heard, and was glad; and the daughters of Judah rejoiced because of your judgments, O LORD.

9 For you, LORD, are high above all the earth: you are exalted far above all gods.

10 You[P] that love the LORD, hate evil: he preserves the souls of his saints; he delivers them out of the hand of the wicked.

11 Light is sown for the righteous, and gladness for the upright in heart.

12 Rejoice in the LORD, you[P] righteous; and give thanks at the remembrance of his holiness.

[A Psalm.]

98 **:1** O sing to the LORD a new song; for he has done marvellous things: his right hand, and his holy arm, has gotten him the victory.

2 The LORD has made known his salvation: his righteousness has he openly showed in the sight of the heathen.

3 He has remembered his mercy and his truth toward the house of Israel: all the ends of the earth have seen the salvation of our God.

4 Make a joyful noise to the LORD, all the earth: make a loud noise, and rejoice, and sing praise.

5 Sing to the LORD with the harp; with the harp, and the voice of a psalm.

6 With trumpets and sound of cornet make a joyful noise before the LORD, the King.

7 Let the sea roar, and the fulness thereof; the world, and they that dwell therein.

8 Let the floods clap their hands: let the hills be joyful together

9 Before the LORD; for he comes to judge the earth: with righteousness shall he judge the world, and the people with equity.

99:1 The LORD reigns; let the people tremble: he sits between the cherubims; let the earth be moved.

2 The LORD is great in Zion; and he is high above all the people.

3 Let them praise your great and terrible name; for it is holy.

4 The king's strength also loves judgment; you do establish equity, you execute judgment and righteousness in Jacob.

5 Exalt you[p] the LORD our God, and worship at his footstool; for he is holy.

6 Moses and Aaron among his priests, and Samuel among them that call upon his name; they called upon the

LORD, and he answered them.

7 He spoke to them in the cloudy pillar: they kept his testimonies, and the ordinance that he gave them.

8 You answered them, O LORD our God: you were a God that forgave them, though you took vengeance of their inventions.

9 Exalt the LORD our God, and worship at his holy hill; for the LORD our God is holy.

[A Psalm of praise.]

100:1 Make a joyful noise to the LORD, all you[P] lands.

2 Serve the LORD with gladness: come before his presence with singing.

3 Know you[P] that the LORD he is God: it is he that has made us, and not we ourselves; we are his people, and the sheep of his pasture.

4 Enter into his gates with thanksgiving, and into his courts with praise: be thankful to him, and bless his name.

5 For the LORD is good; his mercy is everlasting; and his truth endures to all generations.

[A Psalm of praise.]

101:1 I will sing of mercy and judgment: to you, O LORD, will I sing.

2 I will behave myself wisely in a perfect way. O when will you come to me? I will walk within my house with a perfect heart.

3 I will set no wicked thing before my eyes: I hate the work of them that turn aside; it shall not cleave to me.

4 A froward heart shall depart from me: I will not know a wicked person.

5 Whoso privily slanders his neighbor, him will I cut off: him that has a high look and a proud heart will not I suffer.

6 My eyes shall be upon the faithful of the land, that they may dwell with me: he that walks in a perfect way, he shall serve me.

7 He that works deceit shall not dwell within my house: he that tells lies shall not tarry in my sight.

8 I will early destroy all the wicked of the land; that I may cut off all wicked doers from the city of the LORD.

[A Prayer of the afflicted, when he is overwhelmed, and pours out his complaint before the LORD.]

102:1 Hear my prayer, O LORD, and let my cry come to you.

2 Hide not your face from me in the day when I am in trouble; incline your ear to me: in the day when I call answer me speedily.

3 For my days are consumed like smoke, and my bones are burned as a hearth.

4 My heart is smitten, and withered like grass; so that I forget to eat my bread.

5 By reason of the voice of my groaning my bones cleave to my skin.

6 I am like a pelican of the wilderness: I am like an owl of the desert.

7 I watch, and am as a sparrow alone upon the house top.

8 My enemies reproach me all the day; and they that are mad against me are sworn against me.

9 For I have eaten ashes like bread, and mingled my drink with weeping.

10 Because of your indignation and your wrath: for you have lifted me up, and cast me down.

11 My days are like a shadow that declines; and I am withered like grass.

12 But you, O LORD, shall endure for ever; and your remembrance to all generations.

13 You shall arise, and have mercy upon Zion: for the time to favor her, yes, the set time, is come.

14 For your servants take pleasure in her stones, and favor the dust thereof.

15 So the heathen shall fear the name of the LORD, and all the kings of the earth your glory.

16 When the LORD shall build up Zion, he shall appear in his glory.

17 He will regard the prayer of the destitute, and not despise their prayer.

18 This shall be written for the generation to come: and the people which shall be created shall praise the LORD.

19 For he has looked down from the height of his sanctuary; from heaven did the LORD behold the earth;

20 To hear the groaning of the prisoner; to loose those that are appointed to death;

21 To declare the name of the LORD in Zion, and his praise in Jerusalem;

22 When the people are gathered together, and the kingdoms, to serve the LORD.

23 He weakened my strength in the way; he shortened my days.

24 I said, O my God, take me not away in the midst of my days: your years are throughout all generations.

25 Of old have you laid the foundation of the earth: and the heavens are the work of your hands.

26 They shall perish, but you shall endure: yes, all of them shall wax old like a garment; as a vesture shall you change them, and they shall be changed:

27 But you are the same, and your years shall have no end.

28 The children of your servants shall continue, and their seed shall be established before you.

[A Psalm of David.]

103 :1 Bless the LORD, O my soul: and all that is within me, bless his holy name.

2 Bless the LORD, O my soul, and forget not all his benefits:

3 Who forgives all your iniquities; who heals all your diseases;

4 Who redeems your life from destruction; who crowns you with lovingkindness and tender mercies;

5 Who satisfies your mouth with good things; so that your youth is renewed like the eagle's.

6 The LORD executes righteousness and judgment for all that are oppressed.

7 He made known his ways to Moses, his acts to the children of Israel.

8 The LORD is merciful and gracious, slow to anger, and plenteous in mercy.

9 He will not always chide: neither will he keep his anger for ever.

10 He has not dealt with us after our sins; nor rewarded us according to our iniquities.

11 For as the heaven is high above the earth, so great is his mercy toward them that fear him.

12 As far as the east is from the west, so far has he removed our transgressions from us.

13 Like as a father pities his children, so the LORD pities them that fear him.

14 For he knows our frame; he remembers that we are dust.

15 As for man, his days are as grass: as a flower of the field, so he flourishes.

16 For the wind passes over it, and it is gone; and the place thereof shall know it no more.

17 But the mercy of the LORD is from everlasting to everlasting upon them that fear him, and his righteousness to children's children;

18 To such as keep his covenant, and to those that remember his commandments to do them.

19 The LORD has prepared his throne in the heavens; and his kingdom rules over all.

20 Bless the LORD, you[p] his angels, that excel in strength, that do his commandments, hearkening to the voice of his word.

21 Bless you[P] the LORD, all you[P] his hosts; you[P] ministers of his, that do his pleasure.

22 Bless the LORD, all his works in all places of his dominion: bless the LORD, O my soul.

104 :1 Bless the LORD, O my soul. O LORD my God, you are very great; you are clothed with honor and majesty.

2 Who cover yourself with light as with a garment: who stretch out the heavens like a curtain:

3 Who lays the beams of his chambers in the waters: who makes the clouds his chariot: who walks upon the wings of the wind:

4 Who makes his angels spirits; his ministers a flaming fire:

5 Who laid the foundations of the earth, that it should not be removed for ever.

6 You covered it with the deep as with a garment: the waters stood above the mountains.

7 At your rebuke they fled; at the voice of your thunder they hasted away.

8 They go up by the mountains; they go down by the valleys to the place which you have founded for them.

9 You have set a bound that they may not pass over; that they turn not again to cover the earth.

10 He sends the springs into the valleys, which run among the hills.

11 They give drink to every beast of the field: the wild asses quench their thirst.

12 By them shall the fowls of the heaven have their habitation, which sing among the branches.

13 He waters the hills from his chambers: the earth is satisfied with the fruit of your works.

14 He causes the grass to grow for the cattle, and herb for the service of man: that he may bring forth food out of the earth;

15 And wine that makes glad the heart of man, and oil to make his face to shine, and bread which strengthens man's heart.

16 The trees of the LORD are full of sap; the cedars of Lebanon, which he has planted;

17 Where the birds make their nests: as for the stork, the fir trees are her house.

18 The high hills are a refuge for the wild goats; and the rocks for the conies.

19 He appointed the moon for seasons: the sun knows his going down.

20 You make darkness, and it is night: wherein all the beasts of the forest do creep forth.

21 The young lions roar after their prey,

and seek their meat from God.

22 The sun arises, they gather themselves together, and lay them down in their dens.

23 Man goes forth to his work and to his labor until the evening.

24 O LORD, how manifold are your works! in wisdom have you made them all: the earth is full of your riches.

25 So is this great and wide sea, wherein are things creeping innumerable, both small and great beasts.

26 There go the ships: there is that leviathan, whom you have made to play therein.

27 These wait all upon you; that you may give them their meat in due season.

28 That you give them they gather: you open your hand, they are filled with good.

29 You hide your face, they are troubled: you take away their breath, they die, and return to their dust.

30 You send forth your spirit, they are created: and you renew the face of the earth.

31 The glory of the LORD shall endure for ever: the LORD shall rejoice in his works.

32 He looks on the earth, and it trembles: he touches the hills, and they smoke.

33 I will sing to the LORD as long as I live: I will sing praise to my God while I have my being.

34 My meditation of him shall be sweet: I will be glad in the LORD.

35 Let the sinners be consumed out of the earth, and let the wicked be no more. Bless you the LORD, O my soul. Praise you^P the LORD.

105 :1 O give thanks to the LORD; call upon his name: make known his deeds among the people.

2 Sing to him, sing psalms to him: talk you^P of all his wondrous works.

3 Glory you^P in his holy name: let the heart of them rejoice that seek the LORD.

4 Seek the LORD, and his strength: seek his face evermore.

5 Remember his marvellous works that he has done; his wonders, and the judgments of his mouth;

6 O you^P seed of Abraham his servant, you^P children of Jacob his chosen.

7 He is the LORD our God: his judgments are in all the earth.

8 He has remembered his covenant for ever, the word which he commanded to a thousand generations.

9 Which covenant he made with Abraham, and his oath to Isaac;

10 And confirmed the same to Jacob for a law, and to Israel for an everlasting covenant:

11 Saying, _To you will I give the land of Canaan, the lot of your^p inheritance:_

12 When they were but a few men in number; yes, very few, and strangers in it.

13 When they went from one nation to another, from one kingdom to another people;

14 He suffered no man to do them wrong: yes, he reproved kings for their sakes;

15 Saying, _Touch not my anointed, and do my prophets no harm_.

16 Moreover he called for a famine upon the land: he broke the whole staff of bread.

17 He sent a man before them, even Joseph, who was sold for a servant:

18 Whose feet they hurt with fetters: he was laid in iron:

19 Until the time that his word came: the word of the LORD tried him.

20 The king sent and loosed him; even the ruler of the people, and let him go free.

21 He made him lord of his house, and ruler of all his substance:

22 To bind his princes at his pleasure; and teach his senators wisdom.

23 Israel also came into Egypt; and Jacob sojourned in the land of Ham.

24 And he increased his people greatly; and made them stronger than their enemies.

25 He turned their heart to hate his people, to deal subtilly with his servants.

26 He sent Moses his servant; and Aaron whom he had chosen.

27 They showed his signs among them, and wonders in the land of Ham.

28 He sent darkness, and made it dark; and they rebelled not against his word.

29 He turned their waters into blood, and slew their fish.

30 Their land brought forth frogs in abundance, in the chambers of their kings.

31 He spoke, and there came divers sorts of flies, and lice in all their coasts.

32 He gave them hail for rain, and flaming fire in their land.

33 He smote their vines also and their fig trees; and broke the trees of their coasts.

34 He spoke, and the locusts came, and caterpillars, and that without number,

35 And did eat up all the herbs in their land, and devoured the fruit of their ground.

36 He smote also all the firstborn in their land, the chief of all their strength.

37 He brought them forth also with silver and gold: and there was not one feeble person among their tribes.

38 Egypt was glad when they departed: for the fear of them fell upon them.

39 He spread a cloud for a covering; and fire to give light in the night.

40 The people asked, and he brought quails, and satisfied them with the bread of heaven.

41 He opened the rock, and the waters gushed out; they ran in the dry places like a river.

42 For he remembered his holy promise, and Abraham his servant.

43 And he brought forth his people with joy, and his chosen with gladness:

44 And gave them the lands of the heathen: and they inherited the labor of the people;

45 That they might observe his statutes, and keep his laws. Praise you[p] the LORD.

106 :1 Praise you[p] the LORD. O give thanks to the LORD; for he is good: for his mercy endures for ever.

PSALM 106

2 Who can utter the mighty acts of the LORD? who can show forth all his praise?

3 Blessed are they that keep judgment, and he that does righteousness at all times.

4 Remember me, O LORD, with the favor that you bear to your people: O visit me with your salvation;

5 That I may see the good of your chosen, that I may rejoice in the gladness of your nation, that I may glory with your inheritance.

6 We have sinned with our fathers, we have committed iniquity, we have done wickedly.

7 Our fathers understood not your wonders in Egypt; they remembered not the multitude of your mercies; but provoked him at the sea, even at the Red sea.

8 Nevertheless he saved them for his name's sake, that he might make his mighty power to be known.

9 He rebuked the Red sea also, and it was dried up: so he led them through the depths, as through the wilderness.

10 And he saved them from the hand of him that hated them, and redeemed them from the hand of the enemy.

11 And the waters covered their enemies: there was not one of them left.

Books of the Bible—Psalms

12 Then believed they his words;
they sang his praise.

13 They soon forgot his works; they
waited not for his counsel:

14 But lusted exceedingly in the wilderness,
and tempted God in the desert.

15 And he gave them their request;
but sent leanness into their soul.

16 They envied Moses also in the camp,
and Aaron the saint of the LORD.

17 The earth opened and swallowed up Dathan
and covered the company of Abiram.

18 And a fire was kindled in their company;
the flame burned up the wicked.

19 They made a calf in Horeb, and
worshipped the molten image.

20 Thus they changed their glory into the
similitude of an ox that eats grass.

21 They forgot God their savior, which
had done great things in Egypt;

22 Wondrous works in the land of Ham,
and terrible things by the Red sea.

23 Therefore he said that he would destroy
them, had not Moses his chosen stood
before him in the breach, to turn away his
wrath, lest he should destroy them.

24 Yes, they despised the pleasant land, they believed not his word:

25 But murmured in their tents, and hearkened not to the voice of the LORD.

26 Therefore he lifted up his hand against them, to overthrow them in the wilderness:

27 To overthrow their seed also among the nations, and to scatter them in the lands.

28 They joined themselves also to Baalpeor, and ate the sacrifices of the dead.

29 Thus they provoked him to anger with their inventions: and the plague broke in upon them.

30 Then stood up Phinehas, and executed judgment: and so the plague was stayed.

31 And that was counted to him for righteousness to all generations for evermore.

32 They angered him also at the waters of strife, so that it went ill with Moses for their sakes:

33 Because they provoked his spirit, so that he spoke unadvisedly with his lips.

34 They did not destroy the nations, concerning whom the LORD commanded them:

35 But were mingled among the heathen, and learned their works.

36 And they served their idols: which were a snare to them.

37 Yes, they sacrificed their sons
and their daughters to devils,

38 And shed innocent blood, even the blood
of their sons and of their daughters, whom
they sacrificed to the idols of Canaan:
and the land was polluted with blood.

39 Thus were they defiled with their own works,
and went a whoring with their own inventions.

40 Therefore was the wrath of the LORD
kindled against his people, insomuch
that he abhorred his own inheritance.

41 And he gave them into the hand
of the heathen; and they that
hated them ruled over them.

42 Their enemies also oppressed them, and they
were brought into subjection under their hand.

43 Many times did he deliver them; but
they provoked him with their counsel, and
were brought low for their iniquity.

44 Nevertheless he regarded their
affliction, when he heard their cry:

45 And he remembered for them his
covenant, and repented according
to the multitude of his mercies.

46 He made them also to be pitied of all
those that carried them captives.

47 Save us, O LORD our God, and gather us from among the heathen, to give thanks to your holy name, and to triumph in your praise.

48 Blessed be the LORD God of Israel from everlasting to everlasting: and let all the people say, Amen. Praise you[p] the LORD.

107 :1 O give thanks to the LORD, for he is good: for his mercy endures for ever.

2 Let the redeemed of the LORD say so, whom he has redeemed from the hand of the enemy;

3 And gathered them out of the lands, from the east, and from the west, from the north, and from the south.

4 They wandered in the wilderness in a solitary way; they found no city to dwell in.

5 Hungry and thirsty, their soul fainted in them.

6 Then they cried to the LORD in their trouble, and he delivered them out of their distresses.

7 And he led them forth by the right way, that they might go to a city of habitation.

8 Oh that men would praise the LORD for his goodness, and for his wonderful works to the children of men!

9 For he satisfies the longing soul, and fills the hungry soul with goodness.

10 Such as sit in darkness and in the shadow

of death, being bound in affliction and iron;

11 Because they rebelled against
the words of God, and contemned
the counsel of the most High:

12 Therefore he brought down their
heart with labor; they fell down,
and there was none to help.

13 Then they cried to the LORD in their trouble,
and he saved them out of their distresses.

14 He brought them out of darkness
and the shadow of death, and
brake their bands in sunder.

15 Oh that men would praise the LORD
for his goodness, and for his wonderful
works to the children of men!

16 For he has broken the gates of brass,
and cut the bars of iron in sunder.

17 Fools because of their transgression, and
because of their iniquities, are afflicted.

18 Their soul abhors all manner of meat;
and they draw near to the gates of death.

19 Then they cry to the LORD in their trouble,
and he saves them out of their distresses.

20 He sent his word, and healed them, and
delivered them from their destructions.

21 Oh that men would praise the LORD

for his goodness, and for his wonderful works to the children of men!

22 And let them sacrifice the sacrifices of thanksgiving, and declare his works with rejoicing.

23 They that go down to the sea in ships, that do business in great waters;

24 These see the works of the LORD, and his wonders in the deep.

25 For he commands, and raises the stormy wind, which lifts up the waves thereof.

26 They mount up to the heaven, they go down again to the depths: their soul is melted because of trouble.

27 They reel to and fro, and stagger like a drunken man, and are at their wit's end.

28 Then they cry to the LORD in their trouble, and he brings them out of their distresses.

29 He makes the storm a calm, so that the waves thereof are still.

30 Then are they glad because they be quiet; so he brings them to their desired haven.

31 Oh that men would praise the LORD for his goodness, and for his wonderful works to the children of men!

32 Let them exalt him also in the

congregation of the people, and praise
him in the assembly of the elders.

33 He turns rivers into a wilderness, and
the watersprings into dry ground;

34 A fruitful land into barrenness, for the
wickedness of them that dwell therein.

35 He turns the wilderness into a standing
water, and dry ground into watersprings.

36 And there he makes the hungry to dwell,
that they may prepare a city for habitation;

37 And sow the fields, and plant vineyards,
which may yield fruits of increase.

38 He blesses them also, so that they
are multiplied greatly; and suffers
not their cattle to decrease.

39 Again, they are diminished and brought low
through oppression, affliction, and sorrow.

40 He pours contempt upon princes,
and causes them to wander in the
wilderness, where there is no way.

41 Yet sets he the poor on high from affliction,
and makes him families like a flock.

42 The righteous shall see it, and rejoice:
and all iniquity shall stop her mouth.

43 Whoso is wise, and will observe
these things, even they shall understand

PSALM 108

the lovingkindness of the LORD.

[A Song or Psalm of David.]

108 :1 O God, my heart is fixed; I will sing and give praise, even with my glory.

2 Awake, psaltery and harp: I myself will awake early.

3 I will praise you, O LORD, among the people: and I will sing praises to you among the nations.

4 For your mercy is great above the heavens: and your truth reaches to the clouds.

5 Be you exalted, O God, above the heavens: and your glory above all the earth;

6 That your beloved may be delivered: save with your right hand, and answer me.

7 God has spoken in his holiness; *I will rejoice, I will divide Shechem, and mete out the valley of Succoth*.

8 *Gilead is mine; Manasseh is mine; Ephraim also is the strength of my head; Judah is my lawgiver;*

9 *Moab is my washpot; over Edom will I cast out my shoe; over Philistia will I triumph.*

10 Who will bring me into the strong city? who will lead me into Edom?

11 Will not you, O God, who has cast us off? and will not you, O God, go forth with our hosts?

12 Give us help from trouble: for

vain is the help of man.

13 Through God we shall do valiantly: for he it is that shall tread down our enemies.

[To the chief Musician, A Psalm of David.]

109 :1 Hold not your peace, O God of my praise;

2 For the mouth of the wicked and the mouth of the deceitful are opened against me: they have spoken against me with a lying tongue.

3 They compassed me about also with words of hatred; and fought against me without a cause.

4 For my love they are my adversaries: but I give myself to prayer.

5 And they have rewarded me evil for good, and hatred for my love.

6 Set you a wicked man over him: and let Satan stand at his right hand.

7 When he shall be judged, let him be condemned: and let his prayer become sin.

8 Let his days be few; and let another take his office.

9 Let his children be fatherless, and his wife a widow.

10 Let his children be continually vagabonds, and beg: let them seek their bread also out of their desolate places.

11 Let the extortioner catch all that he has; and let the strangers spoil his labor.

12 Let there be none to extend mercy to him: neither let there be any to favor his fatherless children.

13 Let his posterity be cut off; and in the generation following let their name be blotted out.

14 Let the iniquity of his fathers be remembered with the LORD; and let not the sin of his mother be blotted out.

15 Let them be before the LORD continually, that he may cut off the memory of them from the earth.

16 Because that he remembered not to show mercy, but persecuted the poor and needy man, that he might even slay the broken in heart.

17 As he loved cursing, so let it come to him: as he delighted not in blessing, so let it be far from him.

18 As he clothed himself with cursing like as with his garment, so let it come into his bowels like water, and like oil into his bones.

19 Let it be to him as the garment which covers him, and for a girdle wherewith he is girded continually.

20 Let this be the reward of my

adversaries from the LORD, and of them that speak evil against my soul.

21 But do you for me, O God the Lord, for your name's sake: because your mercy is good, deliver you me.

22 For I am poor and needy, and my heart is wounded within me.

23 I am gone like the shadow when it declines: I am tossed up and down as the locust.

24 My knees are weak through fasting; and my flesh fails of fatness.

25 I became also a reproach to them: when they looked upon me they shaked their heads.

26 Help me, O LORD my God: O save me according to your mercy:

27 That they may know that this is your hand; that you, LORD, have done it.

28 Let them curse, but bless you: when they arise, let them be ashamed; but let your servant rejoice.

29 Let my adversaries be clothed with shame, and let them cover themselves with their own confusion, as with a mantle.

30 I will greatly praise the LORD with my mouth; yes, I will praise him among the multitude.

31 For he shall stand at the right

hand of the poor, to save him from those that condemn his soul.

[A Psalm of David.]

110 :1 The Lord said to my LORD, _Sit you at my right hand, until I make your enemies your footstool._

2 The LORD shall send the rod of your strength out of Zion: rule you in the midst of your enemies.

3 Your people shall be willing in the day of your power, in the beauties of holiness from the womb of the morning: you have the dew of your youth.

4 The LORD has sworn, and will not repent, _You are a priest for ever after the order of Melchizedek._

5 The Lord at your right hand shall strike through kings in the day of his wrath.

6 He shall judge among the heathen, he shall fill the places with the dead bodies; he shall wound the heads over many countries.

7 He shall drink of the brook in the way: therefore shall he lift up the head.

111 :1 Praise you[p] the LORD. I will praise the LORD with my whole heart, in the assembly of the upright, and in the congregation.

2 The works of the LORD are great, sought out of all them that have pleasure therein.

3 His work is honorable and glorious: and his righteousness endures for ever.

4 He has made his wonderful works to be remembered: the LORD is gracious and full of compassion.

5 He has given meat to them that fear him: he will ever be mindful of his covenant.

6 He has showed his people the power of his works, that he may give them the heritage of the heathen.

7 The works of his hands are verity and judgment; all his commandments are sure.

8 They stand fast for ever and ever, and are done in truth and uprightness.

9 He sent redemption to his people: he has commanded his covenant for ever: holy and reverend is his name.

10 The fear of the LORD is the beginning of wisdom: a good understanding have all they that do his commandments: his praise endures for ever.

112 :1 Praise you[P] the LORD. Blessed is the man that fears the LORD, that delights greatly in his commandments.

2 His seed shall be mighty upon earth: the generation of the upright shall be blessed.

3 Wealth and riches shall be in his house: and his righteousness endures for ever.

4 To the upright there arises light in the darkness: he is gracious, and full of compassion, and righteous.

5 A good man shows favor, and lends: he will guide his affairs with discretion.

6 Surely he shall not be moved for ever: the righteous shall be in everlasting remembrance.

7 He shall not be afraid of evil tidings: his heart is fixed, trusting in the LORD.

8 His heart is established, he shall not be afraid, until he see his desire upon his enemies.

9 He has dispersed, he has given to the poor; his righteousness endures for ever; his horn shall be exalted with honor.

10 The wicked shall see it, and be grieved; he shall gnash with his teeth, and melt away: the desire of the wicked shall perish.

113 :1 Praise you[P] the LORD. Praise, O you[P] servants of the LORD, praise the name of the LORD.

2 Blessed be the name of the LORD from this time forth and for evermore.

3 From the rising of the sun to the going down of the same the LORD's name is to be praised.

4 The LORD is high above all nations, and his glory above the heavens.

5 Who is like to the LORD our God, who dwells on high,

6 Who humbles himself to behold the things that are in heaven, and in the earth!

7 He raises up the poor out of the dust, and lifts the needy out of the dunghill;

8 That he may set him with princes, even with the princes of his people.

9 He makes the barren woman to keep house, and to be a joyful mother of children. Praise you[p] the LORD.

114 :1 When Israel went out of Egypt, the house of Jacob from a people of strange language;

2 Judah was his sanctuary, and Israel his dominion.

3 The sea saw it, and fled: Jordan was driven back.

4 The mountains skipped like rams,
and the little hills like lambs.

5 What ailed you, O you sea, that you fled?
you Jordan, that you were driven back?

6 You^P mountains, that you^P skipped like
rams; and you^P little hills, like lambs?

7 Tremble, you earth, at the presence of the
Lord, at the presence of the God of Jacob;

8 Which turned the rock into a standing
water, the flint into a fountain of waters.

115 **:1** Not to us, O LORD, not to us,
but to your name give glory, for
your mercy, and for your truth's sake.

2 Wherefore should the heathen
say, Where is now their God?

3 But our God is in the heavens: he has
done whatsoever he has pleased.

4 Their idols are silver and gold,
the work of men's hands.

5 They have mouths, but they speak not:
eyes have they, but they see not:

6 They have ears, but they hear not:
noses have they, but they smell not:

7 They have hands, but they handle not:
feet have they, but they walk not: neither
speak they through their throat.

8 They that make them are like to them; so is every one that trusts in them.

9 O Israel, trust you in the LORD: he is their help and their shield.

10 O house of Aaron, trust in the LORD: he is their help and their shield.

11 You[P] that fear the LORD, trust in the LORD: he is their help and their shield.

12 The LORD has been mindful of us: he will bless us; he will bless the house of Israel; he will bless the house of Aaron.

13 He will bless them that fear the LORD, both small and great.

14 The LORD shall increase you[P] more and more, you[P] and your[P] children.

15 You[P] are blessed of the LORD which made heaven and earth.

16 The heaven, even the heavens, are the LORD's: but the earth has he given to the children of men.

17 The dead praise not the LORD, neither any that go down into silence.

18 But we will bless the Lord from this time forth and for evermore. Praise the Lord.

116 :1 I love the LORD, because he has heard my voice and my supplications.

2 Because he has inclined his ear to me, therefore will I call upon him as long as I live.

3 The sorrows of death compassed me, and the pains of hell got hold upon me: I found trouble and sorrow.

4 Then called I upon the name of the LORD; O LORD, I beseech you, deliver my soul.

5 Gracious is the LORD, and righteous; yes, our God is merciful.

6 The LORD preserves the simple: I was brought low, and he helped me.

7 Return to your rest, O my soul; for the LORD has dealt bountifully with you.

8 For you have delivered my soul from death, my eyes from tears, and my feet from falling.

9 I will walk before the LORD in the land of the living.

10 I believed, therefore have I spoken: I was greatly afflicted:

11 I said in my haste, All men are liars.

12 What shall I render to the LORD for all his benefits toward me?

13 I will take the cup of salvation, and call upon the name of the LORD.

14 I will pay my vows to the LORD now in the presence of all his people.

15 Precious in the sight of the LORD is the death of his saints.

16 O LORD, truly I am your servant; I am your servant, and the son of your handmaid: you have loosed my bonds.

17 I will offer to you the sacrifice of thanksgiving, and will call upon the name of the LORD.

18 I will pay my vows to the LORD now in the presence of all his people.

19 In the courts of the LORD's house, in the midst of you, O Jerusalem. Praise you[P] the LORD.

117:1 O praise the LORD, all you[P] nations: praise him, all you[P] people.

2 For his merciful kindness is great toward us: and the truth of the LORD endures for ever. Praise you[P] the LORD.

118:1 O give thanks to the LORD; for he is good: because his mercy endures for ever.

2 Let Israel now say, that his mercy endures for ever.

3 Let the house of Aaron now say, that his mercy endures for ever.

4 Let them now that fear the LORD say, that his mercy endures for ever.

5 I called upon the LORD in distress: the LORD answered me, and set me in a large place.

6 The LORD is on my side; I will not fear: what can man do to me?

7 The LORD takes my part with them that help me: therefore shall I see my desire upon them that hate me.

8 It is better to trust in the LORD than to put confidence in man.

9 It is better to trust in the LORD than to put confidence in princes.

10 All nations compassed me about: but in the name of the LORD will I destroy them.

11 They compassed me about; yes, they compassed me about: but in the name of the LORD I will destroy them.

12 They compassed me about like bees: they are quenched as the fire of thorns: for in the name of the LORD I will destroy them.

13 You have thrust sore at me that I might fall: but the LORD helped me.

14 The LORD is my strength and song, and is become my salvation.

15 The voice of rejoicing and salvation is

in the tabernacles of the righteous: the right hand of the LORD does valiantly.

16 The right hand of the LORD is exalted: the right hand of the LORD does valiantly.

17 I shall not die, but live, and declare the works of the LORD.

18 The LORD has chastened me sore: but he has not given me over to death.

19 Open to me the gates of righteousness: I will go into them, and I will praise the LORD:

20 This gate of the LORD, into which the righteous shall enter.

21 I will praise you: for you have heard me, and are become my salvation.

22 The stone which the builders refused is become the head stone of the corner.

23 This is the LORD's doing; it is marvellous in our eyes.

24 This is the day which the LORD has made; we will rejoice and be glad in it.

25 Save now, I beseech you, O LORD: O LORD, I beseech you, send now prosperity.

26 Blessed be he that comes in the name of the LORD: we have blessed you[P] out of the house of the LORD.

27 God is the LORD, which has showed

us light: bind the sacrifice with cords, even to the horns of the altar.

28 You are my God, and I will praise you: you are my God, I will exalt you.

29 O give thanks to the LORD; for he is good: for his mercy endures for ever.

119 :1 **ALEPH/ALEF**

Blessed are the undefiled in the way, who walk in the law of the LORD.

2 Blessed are they that keep his testimonies, and that seek him with the whole heart.

3 They also do no iniquity: they walk in his ways.

4 You have commanded us to keep your precepts diligently.

5 O that my ways were directed to keep your statutes!

6 Then shall I not be ashamed, when I have respect to all your commandments.

7 I will praise you with uprightness of heart, when I shall have learned your righteous judgments.

8 I will keep your statutes: O forsake me not utterly.

BET

9 How shall a young man cleanse his way?

by taking heed according to your word.

10 With my whole heart have I sought you: O let me not wander from your commandments.

11 Your word have I hid in my heart, that I might not sin against you.

12 Blessed are you, O LORD: teach me your statutes.

13 With my lips have I declared all the judgments of your mouth.

14 I have rejoiced in the way of your testimonies, as much as in all riches.

15 I will meditate in your precepts, and have respect to your ways.

16 I will delight myself in your statutes: I will not forget your word.

GIMEL

17 Deal bountifully with your servant, that I may live, and keep your word.

18 Open you my eyes, that I may behold wondrous things out of your law.

19 I am a stranger in the earth: hide not your commandments from me.

20 My soul breaks for the longing that it has to your judgments at all times.

21 You have rebuked the proud that are cursed, which do err from your commandments.

22 Remove from me reproach and contempt;
for I have kept your testimonies.

23 Princes also did sit and speak against me:
but your servant did meditate in your statutes.

24 Your testimonies also are my
delight and my counselors.

DALET

25 My soul cleaves to the dust: quicken
you me according to your word.

26 I have declared my ways, and you
heard me: teach me your statutes.

27 Make me to understand the way of your
precepts: so shall I talk of your wondrous works.

28 My soul melts for heaviness: strengthen
you me according to your word.

29 Remove from me the way of lying:
and grant me your law graciously.

30 I have chosen the way of truth: your
judgments have I laid before me.

31 I have stuck to your testimonies:
O LORD, put me not to shame.

32 I will run the way of your commandments,
when you shall enlarge my heart.

HEY/HE

33 Teach me, O LORD, the way of your
statutes; and I shall keep it to the end.

34 Give me understanding, and I shall keep your law; yes, I shall observe it with my whole heart.

35 Make me to go in the path of your commandments; for therein do I delight.

36 Incline my heart to your testimonies, and not to covetousness.

37 Turn away my eyes from beholding vanity; and quicken you me in your way.

38 Establish your word to your servant, who is devoted to your fear.

39 Turn away my reproach which I fear: for your judgments are good.

40 Behold, I have longed after your precepts: quicken me in your righteousness.

WAW/VAV

41 Let your mercies come also to me, O LORD, even your salvation, according to your word.

42 So shall I have wherewith to answer him that reproaches me: for I trust in your word.

43 And take not the word of truth utterly out of my mouth; for I have hoped in your judgments.

44 So shall I keep your law continually for ever and ever.

45 And I will walk at liberty: for I seek your precepts.

46 I will speak of your testimonies also

before kings, and will not be ashamed.

47 And I will delight myself in your commandments, which I have loved.

48 My hands also will I lift up to your commandments, which I have loved; and I will meditate in your statutes.

ZAYIN

49 Remember the word to your servant, upon which you have caused me to hope.

50 This is my comfort in my affliction: for your word has quickened me.

51 The proud have had me greatly in derision: yet have I not declined from your law.

52 I remembered your judgments of old, O LORD; and have comforted myself.

53 Horror has taken hold upon me because of the wicked that forsake your law.

54 Your statutes have been my songs in the house of my pilgrimage.

55 I have remembered your name, O LORD, in the night, and have kept your law.

56 This I had, because I kept your precepts.

HET

57 You are my portion, O LORD: I have said that I would keep your words.

58 I entreated your favor with my whole heart:

be merciful to me according to your word.

59 I thought on my ways, and turned
my feet to your testimonies.

60 I made haste, and delayed not
to keep your commandments.

61 The bands of the wicked have robbed
me: but I have not forgotten your law.

62 At midnight I will rise to give thanks to
you because of your righteous judgments.

63 I am a companion of all them that fear
you, and of them that keep your precepts.

64 The earth, O LORD, is full of your
mercy: teach me your statutes.

TET

65 You have dealt well with your servant,
O LORD, according to your word.

66 Teach me good judgment and knowledge:
for I have believed your commandments.

67 Before I was afflicted I went astray:
but now have I kept your word.

68 You are good, and do good;
teach me your statutes.

69 The proud have forged a lie against me: but
I will keep your precepts with my whole heart.

70 Their heart is as fat as grease;
but I delight in your law.

71 It is good for me that I have been afflicted; that I might learn your statutes.

72 The law of your mouth is better to me than thousands of gold and silver.

YOD

73 Your hands have made me and fashioned me: give me understanding, that I may learn your commandments.

74 They that fear you will be glad when they see me; because I have hoped in your word.

75 I know, O LORD, that your judgments are right, and that you in faithfulness have afflicted me.

76 Let, I pray you, your merciful kindness be for my comfort, according to your word to your servant.

77 Let your tender mercies come to me, that I may live: for your law is my delight.

78 Let the proud be ashamed; for they dealt perversely with me without a cause: but I will meditate in your precepts.

79 Let those that fear you turn to me, and those that have known your testimonies.

80 Let my heart be sound in your statutes; that I be not ashamed.

KAPH/KAF

81 My soul faints for your salvation:
but I hope in your word.

82 My eyes fail for your word, saying,
When will you comfort me?

83 For I am become like a bottle in the
smoke; yet do I not forget your statutes.

84 How many are the days of your
servant? when will you execute judgment
on them that persecute me?

85 The proud have dug pits for me,
which are not after your law.

86 All your commandments are faithful: they
persecute me wrongfully; help you me.

87 They had almost consumed me upon
earth; but I forsook not your precepts.

88 Quicken me after your lovingkindness; so
shall I keep the testimony of your mouth.

LAMED

89 For ever, O LORD, your word
is settled in heaven.

90 Your faithfulness is to all generations: you
have established the earth, and it abides.

91 They continue this day according to your
ordinances: for all are your servants.

92 Unless your law had been my delights, I
should then have perished in my affliction.

93 I will never forget your precepts: for
with them you have quickened me.

94 I am yours, save me: for I
have sought your precepts.

95 The wicked have waited for me to destroy
me: but I will consider your testimonies.

96 I have seen an end of all perfection: but
your commandment is exceeding broad.

MEM

97 O how love I your law! it is
my meditation all the day.

98 You through your commandments
have made me wiser than my enemies:
for they are ever with me.

99 I have more understanding
than all my teachers: for your
testimonies are my meditation.

100 I understand more than the ancients,
because I keep your precepts.

101 I have refrained my feet from every
evil way, that I might keep your word.

102 I have not departed from your
judgments: for you have taught me.

103 How sweet are your words to my taste!
yes, sweeter than honey to my mouth!

104 Through your precepts I get understanding:

therefore I hate every false way.

NUN

105 Your word is a lamp to my
feet, and a light to my path.

106 I have sworn, and I will perform it, that
I will keep your righteous judgments.

107 I am afflicted very much: quicken
me, O LORD, according to your word.

108 Accept, I beseech you, the freewill
offerings of my mouth, O LORD,
and teach me your judgments.

109 My soul is continually in my hand:
yet do I not forget your law.

110 The wicked have laid a snare for me:
yet I erred not from your precepts.

111 Your testimonies have I taken as a heritage
for ever: for they are the rejoicing of my heart.

112 I have inclined my heart to perform
your statutes always, even to the end.

SAMEKH

113 I hate vain thoughts: but your law do I love.

114 You are my hiding place and my
shield: I hope in your word.

115 Depart from me, you[P] evildoers: for I
will keep the commandments of my God.

116 Uphold me according to your

word, that I may live: and let me
not be ashamed of my hope.

117 Hold you me up, and I shall be safe: and I
will have respect to your statutes continually.

118 You have trodden down all them that err
from your statutes: for their deceit is falsehood.

119 You put away all the wicked of the earth
like dross: therefore I love your testimonies.

120 My flesh trembles for fear of you;
and I am afraid of your judgments.

AYIN

121 I have done judgment and justice:
leave me not to my oppressors.

122 Be surety for your servant for good:
let not the proud oppress me.

123 My eyes fail for your salvation, and
for the word of your righteousness.

124 Deal with your servant according to
your mercy, and teach me your statutes.

125 I am your servant; give me understanding,
that I may know your testimonies.

126 It is time for you, LORD, to work:
for they have made void your law.

127 Therefore I love your commandments
above gold; yes, above fine gold.

128 Therefore I esteem all your

precepts concerning all things to be right; and I hate every false way.

PEH/PE

129 Your testimonies are wonderful: therefore does my soul keep them.

130 The entrance of your words gives light; it gives understanding to the simple.

131 I opened my mouth, and panted: for I longed for your commandments.

132 Look you upon me, and be merciful to me, as you use to do to those that love your name.

133 Order my steps in your word: and let not any iniquity have dominion over me.

134 Deliver me from the oppression of man: so will I keep your precepts.

135 Make your face to shine upon your servant; and teach me your statutes.

136 Rivers of waters run down my eyes, because they keep not your law.

TSADE/TSADI

137 Righteous are you, O LORD, and upright are your judgments.

138 Your testimonies that you have commanded are righteous and very faithful.

139 My zeal has consumed me, because my enemies have forgotten your words.

140 Your word is very pure: therefore your servant loves it.

141 I am small and despised: yet do not I forget your precepts.

142 Your righteousness is an everlasting righteousness, and your law is the truth.

143 Trouble and anguish have taken hold on me: yet your commandments are my delights.

144 The righteousness of your testimonies is everlasting: give me understanding, and I shall live.

QOPH/QOF

145 I cried with my whole heart; hear me, O LORD: I will keep your statutes.

146 I cried to you; save me, and I shall keep your testimonies.

147 I prevented the dawning of the morning, and cried: I hoped in your word.

148 My eyes prevent the night watches, that I might meditate in your word.

149 Hear my voice according to your lovingkindness: O LORD, quicken me according to your judgment.

150 They draw nigh that follow after mischief: they are far from your law.

151 You are near, O LORD; and all

your commandments are truth.

152 Concerning your testimonies, I have known of old that you have founded them for ever.

RESH

153 Consider my affliction, and deliver me: for I do not forget your law.

154 Plead my cause, and deliver me: quicken me according to your word.

155 Salvation is far from the wicked: for they seek not your statutes.

156 Great are your tender mercies, O LORD: quicken me according to your judgments.

157 Many are my persecutors and my enemies; yet do I not decline from your testimonies.

158 I beheld the transgressors, and was grieved; because they kept not your word.

159 Consider how I love your precepts: quicken me, O LORD, according to your lovingkindness.

160 Your word is true from the beginning: and every one of your righteous judgments endures for ever.

SHIN

161 Princes have persecuted me without a cause: but my heart stands in awe of your word.

162 I rejoice at your word, as one that finds great spoil.

163 I hate and abhor lying:
but your law do I love.

164 Seven times a day do I praise you
because of your righteous judgments.

165 Great peace have they which love your
law: and nothing shall offend them.

166 LORD, I have hoped for your salvation,
and done your commandments.

167 My soul has kept your testimonies;
and I love them exceedingly.

168 I have kept your precepts and your
testimonies: for all my ways are before you.

TAW/TAV

169 Let my cry come near before you, O LORD:
give me understanding according to your word.

170 Let my supplication come before you:
deliver me according to your word.

171 My lips shall utter praise, when
you have taught me your statutes.

172 My tongue shall speak of your word: for
all your commandments are righteousness.

173 Let your hand help me; for I
have chosen your precepts.

174 I have longed for your salvation, O
LORD; and your law is my delight.

175 Let my soul live, and it shall praise

you; and let your judgments help me.

176 I have gone astray like a lost sheep; seek your servant; for I do not forget your commandments.

[A Song of degrees.]

120:1 In my distress I cried to the LORD, and he heard me.

2 Deliver my soul, O LORD, from lying lips, and from a deceitful tongue.

3 What shall be given to you? or what shall be done to you, you false tongue?

4 Sharp arrows of the mighty, with coals of juniper.

5 Woe is me, that I sojourn in Mesech, that I dwell in the tents of Kedar!

6 My soul has long dwelt with him that hates peace.

7 I am for peace: but when I speak, they are for war.

[A Song of degrees.]

121:1 I will lift up my eyes to the hills, from whence comes my help.

2 My help comes from the Lord, which made heaven and earth.

3 He will not suffer your foot to be moved:

he that keeps you will not slumber.

4 Behold, he that keeps Israel shall neither slumber nor sleep.

5 The LORD is your keeper: the LORD is your shade upon your right hand.

6 The sun shall not smite you by day, nor the moon by night.

7 The LORD shall preserve you from all evil: he shall preserve your soul.

8 The LORD shall preserve your going out and your coming in from this time forth, and even for evermore.

[A Song of degrees of David.]

122:1 I was glad when they said to me, Let us go into the house of the LORD.
2 Our feet shall stand within your gates, O Jerusalem.
3 Jerusalem is built as a city that is compact together:
4 Whither the tribes go up, the tribes of the LORD, to the testimony of Israel, to give thanks to the name of the LORD.
5 For there are set thrones of judgment, the thrones of the house of David.
6 Pray for the peace of Jerusalem: they shall prosper that love you.

7 Peace be within your walls, and prosperity within your palaces.

8 For my brethren and companions' sakes, I will now say, Peace be within you.

9 Because of the house of the LORD our God I will seek your good.

[A Song of degrees.]

123 :1 To you lift I up my eyes, O you that dwell in the heavens.

2 Behold, as the eyes of servants look to the hand of their masters, and as the eyes of a maiden to the hand of her mistress; so our eyes wait upon the LORD our God, until that he have mercy upon us.

3 Have mercy upon us, O LORD, have mercy upon us: for we are exceedingly filled with contempt.

4 Our soul is exceedingly filled with the scorning of those that are at ease, and with the contempt of the proud.

[A Song of degrees of David.]

124 :1 If it had not been the LORD who was on our side, now may Israel say;

2 If it had not been the LORD who was on our side, when men rose up against us:

3 Then they had swallowed us up quick,
when their wrath was kindled against us:

4 Then the waters had overwhelmed us,
the stream had gone over our soul:

5 Then the proud waters had gone over our soul.

6 Blessed be the LORD, who has not
given us as a prey to their teeth.

7 Our soul is escaped as a bird out of
the snare of the fowlers: the snare
is broken, and we are escaped.

8 Our help is in the name of the LORD,
who made heaven and earth.

[A Song of degrees.]

125:1 They that trust in the LORD shall
be as mount Zion, which cannot
be removed, but abides for ever.

2 As the mountains are round about
Jerusalem, so the LORD is round about his
people from henceforth even for ever.

3 For the rod of the wicked shall not rest
upon the lot of the righteous; lest the
righteous put forth their hands to iniquity.

4 Do good, O LORD, to those that be good,
and to them that are upright in their hearts.

5 As for such as turn aside to their
crooked ways, the LORD shall lead

them forth with the workers of iniquity:
but peace shall be upon Israel.

[A Song of degrees.]

126:1 When the LORD turned
again the captivity of Zion,
we were like them that dream.

2 Then was our mouth filled with laughter,
and our tongue with singing: then said
they among the heathen, The LORD
has done great things for them.

3 The LORD has done great things
for us; whereof we are glad.

4 Turn again our captivity, O LORD,
as the streams in the south.

5 They that sow in tears shall reap in joy.

6 He that goes forth and weeps, bearing
precious seed, shall doubtless come again
with rejoicing, bringing his sheaves with him.

[A Song of degrees for Solomon.]

127:1 Except the LORD build the
house, they labor in vain that
build it: except the LORD keep the city,
the watchman wakes but in vain.

2 It is vain for you^p to rise up early, to
sit up late, to eat the bread of sorrows:

for so he gives his beloved sleep.

3 Lo, children are a heritage of the LORD: and the fruit of the womb is his reward.

4 As arrows are in the hand of a mighty man; so are children of the youth.

5 Happy is the man that has his quiver full of them: they shall not be ashamed, but they shall speak with the enemies in the gate.

[A Song of degrees.]

128:1 Blessed is every one that fears the LORD; that walks in his ways.

2 For you shall eat the labor of your hands: happy shall you be, and it shall be well with you.

3 Your wife shall be as a fruitful vine by the sides of your house: your children like olive plants round about your table.

4 Behold, that thus shall the man be blessed that fears the LORD.

5 The LORD shall bless you out of Zion: and you shall see the good of Jerusalem all the days of your life.

6 Yes, you shall see your children's children, and peace upon Israel.

[A Song of degrees.]

129 :1 Many a time have they afflicted me from my youth, may Israel now say:

2 Many a time have they afflicted me from my youth: yet they have not prevailed against me.

3 The plowers plowed upon my back: they made long their furrows.

4 The LORD is righteous: he has cut asunder the cords of the wicked.

5 Let them all be confounded and turned back that hate Zion.

6 Let them be as the grass upon the housetops, which withers before it grows up:

7 Wherewith the mower fills not his hand; nor he that binds sheaves his bosom.

8 Neither do they which go by say, The blessing of the LORD be upon you[P]: we bless you[P] in the name of the Lord.

[A Song of degrees.]

130 :1 Out of the depths have I cried to you, O LORD.

2 Lord, hear my voice: let your ears be attentive to the voice of my supplications.

3 If you, LORD, should mark iniquities, O Lord, who shall stand?

4 But there is forgiveness with
you, that you may be feared.

5 I wait for the LORD, my soul does
wait, and in his word do I hope.

6 My soul waits for the Lord more than they
that watch for the morning: I say, more
than they that watch for the morning.

7 Let Israel hope in the LORD: for
with the Lord there is mercy, and with
him is plenteous redemption.

8 And he shall redeem Israel
from all his iniquities.

[A Song of degrees of David.]

131:1 LORD, my heart is not haughty, nor my
eyes lofty: neither do I exercise myself
in great matters, or in things too high for me.

2 Surely I have behaved and quieted myself,
as a child that is weaned of his mother:
my soul is even as a weaned child.

3 Let Israel hope in the LORD from
henceforth and for ever.

[A Song of degrees.]

132:1 LORD, remember David,
and all his afflictions:

2 How he swore to the LORD, and

vowed to the mighty God of Jacob;

3 Surely I will not come into the tabernacle of my house, nor go up into my bed;

4 I will not give sleep to my eyes, or slumber to my eyelids,

5 Until I find out a place for the Lord, a habitation for the mighty God of Jacob.

6 Lo, we heard of it at Ephratah: we found it in the fields of the wood.

7 We will go into his tabernacles: we will worship at his footstool.

8 Arise, O LORD, into your rest; you, and the ark of your strength.

9 Let your priests be clothed with righteousness; and let your saints shout for joy.

10 For your servant David's sake turn not away the face of your anointed.

11 The LORD has sworn in truth to David; he will not turn from it; *Of the fruit of your body will I set upon your throne.*

12 *If your children will keep my covenant and my testimony that I shall teach them, their children shall also sit upon your throne for evermore.*

13 For the LORD has chosen Zion; he has desired it for his habitation.

14 *This is my rest for ever: here will*

I dwell; for I have desired it.

15 *I will abundantly bless her provision:*
I will satisfy her poor with bread.

16 *I will also clothe her priests with salvation:*
and her saints shall shout aloud for joy.

17 *There will I make the horn of David to bud:*
I have ordained a lamp for my anointed.

18 *His enemies will I clothe with shame:*
but upon himself shall his crown flourish.

[A Song of degrees of David.]

133:1 Behold, how good and how pleasant it is for brethren to dwell together in unity!

2 It is like the precious ointment upon the head, that ran down upon the beard, even Aaron's beard: that went down to the skirts of his garments;

3 As the dew of Hermon, and as the dew that descended upon the mountains of Zion: for there the LORD commanded the blessing, even life for evermore.

[A Song of degrees.]

134:1 Behold, bless you*ᵖ* the LORD, all you*ᵖ* servants of the LORD, which by night stand in the house of the LORD.

2 Lift up your*ᵖ* hands in the

sanctuary, and bless the LORD.

3 The LORD that made heaven and earth bless you out of Zion.

135 :1 Praise you[P] the LORD. Praise you[P] the name of the LORD; praise him, O you[P] servants of the LORD.

2 You[P] that stand in the house of the LORD, in the courts of the house of our God.

3 Praise the LORD; for the LORD is good: sing praises to his name; for it is pleasant.

4 For the LORD has chosen Jacob to himself, and Israel for his peculiar treasure.

5 For I know that the LORD is great, and that our Lord is above all gods.

6 Whatsoever the LORD pleased, that did he in heaven, and in earth, in the seas, and all deep places.

7 He causes the vapors to ascend from the ends of the earth; he makes lightnings for the rain; he brings the wind out of his treasuries.

8 Who smote the firstborn of Egypt, both of man and beast.

9 Who sent tokens and wonders into the midst of you, O Egypt, upon Pharaoh, and upon all his servants.

10 Who smote great nations,

and slew mighty kings;

11 Sihon king of the Amorites, and Og king of Bashan, and all the kingdoms of Canaan:

12 And gave their land for a heritage, a heritage to Israel his people.

13 Your name, O LORD, endures for ever; and your memorial, O LORD, throughout all generations.

14 For the LORD will judge his people, and he will repent himself concerning his servants.

15 The idols of the heathen are silver and gold, the work of men's hands.

16 They have mouths, but they speak not; eyes have they, but they see not;

17 They have ears, but they hear not; neither is there any breath in their mouths.

18 They that make them are like to them: so is every one that trusts in them.

19 Bless the LORD, O house of Israel: bless the LORD, O house of Aaron:

20 Bless the LORD, O house of Levi: you[p] that fear the LORD, bless the LORD.

21 Blessed be the LORD out of Zion, which dwells at Jerusalem. Praise you[p] the LORD.

136:1 O give thanks to the LORD; for he is good: for his mercy endures for ever.

2 O give thanks to the God of gods: for his mercy endures for ever.

3 O give thanks to the Lord of lords: for his mercy endures for ever.

4 To him who alone does great wonders: for his mercy endures for ever.

5 To him that by wisdom made the heavens: for his mercy endures for ever.

6 To him that stretched out the earth above the waters: for his mercy endures for ever.

7 To him that made great lights: for his mercy endures for ever:

8 The sun to rule by day: for his mercy endures for ever:

9 The moon and stars to rule by night: for his mercy endures for ever.

10 To him that smote Egypt in their firstborn: for his mercy endures for ever:

11 And brought out Israel from among them: for his mercy endures for ever:

12 With a strong hand, and with a stretched out arm: for his mercy endures for ever.

13 To him which divided the Red sea into parts: for his mercy endures for ever:

14 And made Israel to pass through the midst of it: for his mercy endures for ever:

15 But overthrew Pharaoh and his host in the Red sea: for his mercy endures for ever.

16 To him which led his people through the wilderness: for his mercy endures for ever.

17 To him which smote great kings: for his mercy endures for ever:

18 And slew famous kings: for his mercy endures for ever:

19 Sihon king of the Amorites: for his mercy endures for ever:

20 And Og the king of Bashan: for his mercy endures for ever:

21 And gave their land for a heritage: for his mercy endures for ever:

22 Even a heritage to Israel his servant: for his mercy endures for ever.

23 Who remembered us in our low estate: for his mercy endures for ever:

24 And has redeemed us from our enemies: for his mercy endures for ever.

25 Who gives food to all flesh: for his mercy endures for ever.

26 O give thanks to the God of heaven: for his mercy endures for ever.

137

:1 By the rivers of Babylon, there we sat down, yes, we wept, when we remembered Zion.

2 We hanged our harps upon the willows in the midst thereof.

3 For there they that carried us away captive required of us a song; and they that wasted us required of us mirth, saying, Sing us one of the songs of Zion.

4 How shall we sing the LORD's song in a strange land?

5 If I forget you, O Jerusalem, let my right hand forget her cunning.

6 If I do not remember you, let my tongue cleave to the roof of my mouth; if I prefer not Jerusalem above my chief joy.

7 Remember, O LORD, the children of Edom in the day of Jerusalem; who said, Rase it, rase it, even to the foundation thereof.

8 O daughter of Babylon, who are to be destroyed; happy shall he be, that rewards you as you have served us.

9 Happy shall he be, that takes and dashes your little ones against the stones.

[A Psalm of David.]

138 :1 I will praise you with my whole heart: before the gods will I sing praise to you.

2 I will worship toward your holy temple, and praise your name for your lovingkindness and for your truth: for you have magnified your word above all your name.

3 In the day when I cried you answered me, and strengthened me with strength in my soul.

4 All the kings of the earth shall praise you, O LORD, when they hear the words of your mouth.

5 Yes, they shall sing in the ways of the LORD: for great is the glory of the LORD.

6 Though the LORD be high, yet has he respect to the lowly: but the proud he knows afar off.

7 Though I walk in the midst of trouble, you will revive me: you shall stretch forth your hand against the wrath of my enemies, and your right hand shall save me.

8 The LORD will perfect that which concerns me: your mercy, O LORD, endures for ever: forsake not the works of your own hands.

[To the chief Musician, A Psalm of David.]

139 :1 O LORD, you have searched me, and known me.

2 You know my downsitting and my uprising,

you understand my thought afar off.

3 You compass my path and my lying down, and are acquainted with all my ways.

4 For there is not a word in my tongue, but, lo, O LORD, you know it altogether.

5 You have beset me behind and before, and laid your hand upon me.

6 Such knowledge is too wonderful for me; it is high, I cannot attain to it.

7 Where shall I go from your spirit? or where shall I flee from your presence?

8 If I ascend up into heaven, you are there: if I make my bed in hell, behold, you are there.

9 If I take the wings of the morning, and dwell in the uttermost parts of the sea;

10 Even there shall your hand lead me, and your right hand shall hold me.

11 If I say, Surely the darkness shall cover me; even the night shall be light about me.

12 Yes, the darkness hides not from you; but the night shines as the day: the darkness and the light are both alike to you.

13 For you have possessed my reins: you have covered me in my mother's womb.

14 I will praise you; for I am fearfully and wonderfully made: marvellous are your works; and that my soul knows right well.

15 My substance was not hid from you, when I was made in secret, and curiously wrought in the lowest parts of the earth.

16 Your eyes did see my substance, yet being unperfect; and in your book all my members were written, which in continuance were fashioned, when as yet there was none of them.

17 How precious also are your thoughts to me, O God! how great is the sum of them!

18 If I should count them, they are more in number than the sand: when I awake, I am still with you.

19 Surely you will slay the wicked, O God: depart from me therefore, you[p] bloody men.

20 For they speak against you wickedly, and your enemies take your name in vain.

21 Do not I hate them, O LORD, that hate you? and am not I grieved with those that rise up against you?

22 I hate them with perfect hatred: I count them my enemies.

23 Search me, O God, and know my heart: try me, and know my thoughts:

24 And see if there be any wicked way in me, and lead me in the way everlasting.

[To the chief Musician, A Psalm of David.]

140 :1 Deliver me, O LORD, from the evil man: preserve me from the violent man;

2 Which imagine mischiefs in their heart; continually are they gathered together for war.

3 They have sharpened their tongues like a serpent; adders' poison is under their lips. Selah.

4 Keep me, O LORD, from the hands of the wicked; preserve me from the violent man; who have purposed to overthrow my goings.

5 The proud have hid a snare for me, and cords; they have spread a net by the wayside; they have set gins for me. Selah.

6 I said to the LORD, You are my God: hear the voice of my supplications, O Lord.

7 O God the Lord, the strength of my salvation, you have covered my head in the day of battle.

8 Grant not, O Lord, the desires of the wicked: further not his wicked device; lest they exalt themselves. Selah.

9 As for the head of those that compass me about, let the mischief of their own lips cover them.

10 Let burning coals fall upon them: let them be cast into the fire; into deep pits, that they rise not up again.

11 Let not an evil speaker be established in the earth: evil shall hunt the violent man to overthrow him.

12 I know that the LORD will maintain the cause of the afflicted, and the right of the poor.

13 Surely the righteous shall give thanks to your name: the upright shall dwell in your presence.

[A Psalm of David.]

141 :1 LORD, I cry to you: make haste to me; give ear to my voice, when I cry to you.

2 Let my prayer be set forth before you as incense; and the lifting up of my hands as the evening sacrifice.

3 Set a watch, O LORD, before my mouth; keep the door of my lips.

4 Incline not my heart to any evil thing, to practice wicked works with men that work iniquity: and let me not eat of their dainties.

5 Let the righteous smite me; it shall be a kindness: and let him reprove me; it shall be an excellent oil, which shall not break my head: for yet my prayer also shall be in their calamities.

6 When their judges are overthrown in stony places, they shall hear my words; for they are sweet.

7 Our bones are scattered at the grave's mouth, as when one cuts and cleaves wood upon the earth.

8 But my eyes are to you, O God the Lord: in you is my trust; leave not my soul destitute.

9 Keep me from the snares which they have laid for me, and the gins of the workers of iniquity.

10 Let the wicked fall into their own nets, while that I withal escape.

[Maschil of David; A Prayer when he was in the cave.]

142:1 I cried to the LORD with my voice; with my voice to the LORD did I make my supplication.

2 I poured out my complaint before him; I showed before him my trouble.

3 When my spirit was overwhelmed within me, then you knew my path. In the way wherein I walked have they privily laid a snare for me.

4 I looked on my right hand, and beheld, but there was no man that would know me: refuge failed me; no man cared for my soul.

5 I cried to you, O LORD: I said, You are my refuge and my portion in the land of the living.

6 Attend to my cry; for I am brought very low: deliver me from my persecutors;

for they are stronger than I.

7 Bring my soul out of prison, that I may praise your name: the righteous shall compass me about; for you shall deal bountifully with me.

[A Psalm of David.]

143:1 Hear my prayer, O LORD, give ear to my supplications: in your faithfulness answer me, and in your righteousness.

2 And enter not into judgment with your servant: for in your sight shall no man living be justified.

3 For the enemy has persecuted my soul; he has smitten my life down to the ground; he has made me to dwell in darkness, as those that have been long dead.

4 Therefore is my spirit overwhelmed within me; my heart within me is desolate.

5 I remember the days of old; I meditate on all your works; I muse on the work of your hands.

6 I stretch forth my hands to you: my soul thirsts after you, as a thirsty land. Selah.

7 Hear me speedily, O LORD: my spirit fails: hide not your face from me, lest I be like to them that go down into the pit.

8 Cause me to hear your lovingkindness in the morning; for in you do I trust: cause me to know the way wherein I should walk; for I lift up my soul to you.

9 Deliver me, O LORD, from my enemies: I flee to you to hide me.

10 Teach me to do your will; for you are my God: your spirit is good; lead me into the land of uprightness.

11 Quicken me, O LORD, for your name's sake: for your righteousness' sake bring my soul out of trouble.

12 And of your mercy cut off my enemies, and destroy all them that afflict my soul: for I am your servant.

[A Psalm of David.]

144:1 Blessed be the LORD my strength which teaches my hands to war, and my fingers to fight:

2 My goodness, and my fortress; my high tower, and my deliverer; my shield, and he in whom I trust; who subdues my people under me.

3 LORD, what is man, that you takest knowledge of him! or the son of man, that you make account of him!

4 Man is like to vanity: his days are as a shadow that passes away.

5 Bow your heavens, O LORD, and come down:

touch the mountains, and they shall smoke.

6 Cast forth lightning, and scatter them:
shoot out your arrows, and destroy them.

7 Send your hand from above; rid me,
and deliver me out of great waters,
from the hand of strange children;

8 Whose mouth speaks vanity, and their
right hand is a right hand of falsehood.

9 I will sing a new song to you, O God:
upon a psaltery and an instrument of
ten strings will I sing praises to you.

10 It is he that gives salvation
to kings: who delivers David his
servant from the hurtful sword.

11 Rid me, and deliver me from the hand of
strange children, whose mouth speaks vanity,
and their right hand is a right hand of falsehood:

12 That our sons may be as plants grown
up in their youth; that our daughters
may be as corner stones, polished
after the similitude of a palace:

13 That our garners may be full, affording all
manner of store: that our sheep may bring forth
thousands and ten thousands in our streets:

14 That our oxen may be strong to labor;
that there be no breaking in, nor going out;
that there be no complaining in our streets.

15 Happy is that people, that is
in such a case: yes, happy is that
people, whose God is the LORD.

[David's Psalm of praise.]

145:1 I will extol you, my God, O king; and
I will bless your name for ever and ever.

2 Every day will I bless you; and I will
praise your name for ever and ever.

3 Great is the LORD, and greatly to be
praised; and his greatness is unsearchable.

4 One generation shall praise your works to
another, and shall declare your mighty acts.

5 I will speak of the glorious honor of your
majesty, and of your wondrous works.

6 And men shall speak of the might of your
terrible acts: and I will declare your greatness.

7 They shall abundantly utter the
memory of your great goodness, and
shall sing of your righteousness.

8 The LORD is gracious, and full of compassion;
slow to anger, and of great mercy.

9 The LORD is good to all: and his tender
mercies are over all his works.

10 All your works shall praise you, O
LORD; and your saints shall bless you.

11 They shall speak of the glory of your

kingdom, and talk of your power;

12 To make known to the sons of
men his mighty acts, and the glorious
majesty of his kingdom.

13 Your kingdom is an everlasting
kingdom, and your dominion endures
throughout all generations.

14 The LORD upholds all that fall, and
raises up all those that be bowed down.

15 The eyes of all wait upon you; and you
give them their meat in due season.

16 You open your hand, and satisfy
the desire of every living thing.

17 The LORD is righteous in all his
ways, and holy in all his works.

18 The LORD is nigh to all them that call
upon him, to all that call upon him in truth.

19 He will fulfill the desire of them that fear him:
he also will hear their cry, and will save them.

20 The LORD preserves all them that love
him: but all the wicked will he destroy.

21 My mouth shall speak the praise
of the LORD: and let all flesh bless
his holy name for ever and ever.

146 :1 Praise you[p] the LORD. Praise
the LORD, O my soul.

2 While I live will I praise the LORD: I will sing praises to my God while I have any being.

3 Put not your[p] trust in princes, nor in the son of man, in whom there is no help.

4 His breath goes forth, he returns to his earth; in that very day his thoughts perish.

5 Happy is he that has the God of Jacob for his help, whose hope is in the LORD his God:

6 Which made heaven, and earth, the sea, and all that therein is: which keeps truth for ever:

7 Which executes judgment for the oppressed: which gives food to the hungry. The LORD looses the prisoners:

8 The LORD opens the eyes of the blind: the LORD raises them that are bowed down: the LORD loves the righteous:

9 The LORD preserves the strangers; he relieves the fatherless and widow: but the way of the wicked he turns upside down.

10 The LORD shall reign for ever, even your God, O Zion, to all generations. Praise you[p] the LORD.

147 :1 Praise you[p] the LORD: for it is good to sing praises to our God; for it is pleasant; and praise is comely.

2 The LORD does build up Jerusalem: he gathers together the outcasts of Israel.

3 He heals the broken in heart,
and binds up their wounds.

4 He tells the number of the stars;
he calls them all by their names.

5 Great is our Lord, and of great power:
his understanding is infinite.

6 The LORD lifts up the meek: he casts
the wicked down to the ground.

7 Sing to the LORD with thanksgiving;
sing praise upon the harp to our God:

8 Who covers the heaven with clouds, who
prepares rain for the earth, who makes
grass to grow upon the mountains.

9 He gives to the beast his food, and
to the young ravens which cry.

10 He delights not in the strength of the horse:
he takes not pleasure in the legs of a man.

11 The LORD takes pleasure in them that
fear him, in those that hope in his mercy.

12 Praise the LORD, O Jerusalem;
praise your God, O Zion.

13 For he has strengthened the bars of your
gates; he has blessed your children within you.

14 He makes peace in your borders, and
fills you with the finest of the wheat.

15 He sends forth his commandment upon

earth: his word runs very swiftly.

16 He gives snow like wool: he scatters the hoarfrost like ashes.

17 He casts forth his ice like morsels: who can stand before his cold?

18 He sends out his word, and melts them: he causes his wind to blow, and the waters flow.

19 He shows his word to Jacob, his statutes and his judgments to Israel.

20 He has not dealt so with any nation: and as for his judgments, they have not known them. Praise you[p] the LORD.

148 **:1** Praise you[p] the LORD. Praise you[p] the LORD from the heavens: praise him in the heights.

2 Praise you[p] him, all his angels: praise you[p] him, all his hosts.

3 Praise you[p] him, sun and moon: praise him, all you[p] stars of light.

4 Praise him, you[p] heavens of heavens, and you[p] waters that be above the heavens.

5 Let them praise the name of the LORD: for he commanded, and they were created.

6 He has also established them for ever and ever: he has made a decree which shall not pass.

7 Praise the LORD from the earth, you[p] dragons, and all deeps:

8 Fire, and hail; snow, and vapors; stormy wind fulfilling his word:

9 Mountains, and all hills; fruitful trees, and all cedars:

10 Beasts, and all cattle; creeping things, and flying fowl:

11 Kings of the earth, and all people; princes, and all judges of the earth:

12 Both young men, and maidens; old men, and children:

13 Let them praise the name of the LORD: for his name alone is excellent; his glory is above the earth and heaven.

14 He also exalts the horn of his people, the praise of all his saints; even of the children of Israel, a people near to him. Praise you[p] the LORD.

149 :1 Praise you[p] the LORD. Sing to the LORD a new song, and his praise in the congregation of saints.

2 Let Israel rejoice in him that made him: let the children of Zion be joyful in their King.

3 Let them praise his name in the dance: let them sing praises to him with the timbrel and harp.

4 For the LORD takes pleasure in his people: he will beautify the meek with salvation.

5 Let the saints be joyful in glory: let them sing aloud upon their beds.

6 Let the high praises of God be in their mouth, and a two-edged sword in their hand;

7 To execute vengeance upon the heathen, and punishments upon the people;

8 To bind their kings with chains, and their nobles with fetters of iron;

9 To execute upon them the judgment written: this honor have all his saints. Praise you[p] the LORD.

150 :1 Praise you[p] the LORD. Praise God in his sanctuary: praise him in the firmament of his power.

2 Praise him for his mighty acts: praise him according to his excellent greatness.

3 Praise him with the sound of the trumpet: praise him with the psaltery and harp.

4 Praise him with the timbrel and dance: praise him with stringed instruments and organs.

5 Praise him upon the loud cymbals: praise him upon the high sounding cymbals.

6 Let every thing that has breath praise the Lord. Praise you[p] the LORD.

Books of the Bible—Psalms

Guides for finding a Psalm

By Organized Topic:

1. Didactic *[teaching, precepts, principles, rules]*

(1) Good and bad men: Psalm 1, 5, 7, 9-12, 14, 15, 17, 24, 25, 32, 34, 36, 37, 50, 52, 53, 58, 73, 75, 84, 91, 92, 94, 112, 121, 125, 127, 128, 133;

(2) God's law: Psalm 19, 119;

(3) Human life: Psalm 39, 49, 90;

(4) Duty of rulers: Psalm 82, 101.

2. Praise

(1) For God's goodness generally to Israel: Psalm 46, 48, 65, 66, 68, 76, 81, 85, 98, 105, 124, 126, 129, 135, 136, 149;

(2) To good men: Psalm 23, 34, 36, 91, 100, 103, 107, 117, 121, 145, 146;

(3) Mercies to individuals: Psalm 9, 18, 22, 30, 40, 75, 103, 108, 116, 118, 138, 144;

(4) For His attributes generally: Psalm 8, 19, 24, 29, 33, 47, 50, 65, 66, 76, 77, 93, 95-97, 99, 104, 111, 113-115, 134, 139, 147, 148, 150.

3. Devotion (Expresses)

(1) Penitence: Psalm 6, 25, 32, 38, 51, 102, 130, 143;

(2) Trust in trouble: Psalm 3, 16, 27, 31, 54, 56, 57, 61, 62, 71, 86;

(3) Sorrow with hope: Psalm

13, 22, 69, 77, 88;

(4) Of deep distress: Psalm 4, 5, 11, 28, 41, 55, 59, 64, 70, 109, 120, 140, 141, 143;

(5) Feelings when deprived of religious privileges: Psalm 42, 43, 63, 84;

(6) Desire for help: Psalm 7, 17, 26, 35, 44, 60, 74, 79, 80, 83, 89, 94, 102, 129, 137;

(7) Intercession: Psalm 20, 67, 122, 132, 144.

4. Historical Psalm 78, 105, 106.

5. Prophetical 2, 16, 22, 40, 45, 68, 69, 72, 97, 110, 118.

By Subject/Theme:

Communion preparation: Psalm 23, 25, 26, 36, 41, 43, 63, 84, 85, 86, 122, 130, 133, 139.

Communion thanksgiving: Psalm 8, 15, 18, 19, 27, 29, 30, 34, 100, 103, 110, 118, 145, 150.

God our Creator: Psalm 8, 19, 33, 65, 111, 104, 145, 147.

God our refuge: Psalm 4, 17, 20, 37, 46, 49, 54, 61, 71, 91, 103, 121, 146.

God the Judge: Psalm 1, 7, 11, 46, 50, 62, 75, 76, 82, 90, 96, 97, 98.

God the Redeemer: Psalm 15, 33, 102, 103, 111, 113, 114, 126, 130, 138.

God's Divine Guidance: Psalm

25, 43, 80, 85, 111, 112.

God's Glory: Psalm 18, 29, 99, 36, 46, 148, 150.

God's Law: Psalm 19, 50, 62, 111, 119, 147. 23, 33, 34, 37, 89, 121, 124, 139, 145, 146, 147.

God's Mercy: Psalm 23, 32, 57, 61, 62, 63, 73, 77, 85, 86, 100, 103, 118, 130, 145.

God's Sovereignty: Psalm 24, 46, 47, 72, 89, 93, 96, 97, 98, 99, 112, 146, 145.

God's Wisdom: Psalm 33, 104, 111, 113, 139, 145, 147.

Prayer: Psalm 4, 5, 17, 20, 28, 31, 54, 61, 84, 86, 102, 141, 142.

In Times of Trouble: Psalm 3, 11, 12, 13, 18, 20, 30, 40, 46, 49, 57, 62, 63, 80, 85, 86, 90, 107, 118, 144, 146.

Our Transitory Life: Psalm 39, 49, 90, 102.

Peace: Psalm 29, 46, 76, 85, 98, 100, 124, 125, 126.

Penitential Psalms: Psalm 6, 32, 38, 51, 102, 130, 143.

Righteousness: Psalm 1, 11, 12, 15, 18, 19, 26, 34, 40, 92, 111, 112.

Thanksgiving: Psalm 30, 65, 67, 92, 98, 100, 111, 103, 107, 116, 134, 138, 145, 147, 148, 150.

The Church: Psalm 46, 48,

84, 111, 122, 133, 147.

The Incarnation: Psalm 2, 8, 85, 89, 102, 110, 111, 113, 132.

The Passion: Psalm 22, 40, 42, 54, 69, 88, 116, 130.

The Hope of Immortality: Psalm 16, 30, 42, 49, 66, 73, 103, 116, 121, 139, 146.

Trust in God: Psalm 27, 31, 57, 62, 63, 71, 73, 77, 91, 118, 121, 123, 124, 125, 143, 146.

Worship: Psalm 5, 26, 43, 63, 65, 66, 67, 84, 96, 100, 102, 116, 122, 138.

Repeated words and phrases you could mark in Psalms:

- acts
- adversaries
- affliction
- among
- anger
- anointed
- arm
- as for
- ashamed
- away
- be glad
- become
- bless the LORD
- blessed
- born
- brought forth
- call upon
- chosen
- coals
- commandments
- compassed
- continually
- covenant
- days
- deep
- defense
- deliver
- destroy
- distress(es)
- earth
- endures
- enemy/enemies
- evil
- exalted
- face to shine
- faithfulness
- far from
- fear/feared
- flourish
- for ever/forever
- fret
- fulness thereof
- give thanks
- glory

- ❏ goodness
- ❏ grave
- ❏ hate
- ❏ he is good
- ❏ heart
- ❏ heaven(s)
- ❏ help
- ❏ heritage
- ❏ his mercy
  endures forever
- ❏ Holy
- ❏ hosts
- ❏ house of the LORD
- ❏ hungry
- ❏ I will
- ❏ in your courts
- ❏ iniquity
- ❏ joyful/joyful noise
- ❏ judgments
- ❏ King
- ❏ law
- ❏ let/let them/let us
- ❏ like
- ❏ lips

- ❏ long
- ❏ make(s)
- ❏ may be
- ❏ me
- ❏ meditate
- ❏ mercy
- ❏ mighty
- ❏ most high
- ❏ name
- ❏ needy
- ❏ neighbor(s)
- ❏ no
- ❏ O give thanks
- ❏ only
- ❏ our God
- ❏ out
- ❏ pay my/your vows
- ❏ people
- ❏ perish
- ❏ poor
- ❏ praise
- ❏ precepts
- ❏ provoked
- ❏ quicken

- refuge
- rejoice
- remember
- reproach
- right
- right hand
- righteous(ness)
- rock
- saints
- salvation
- seed
- Selah
- shall
- shield
- shoot
- should have
- shout for joy
- sing
- sing praises
- Zion
- sore
- soul
- statues
- strong
- tender mercies
- testimonies
- this generation
- throne
- trouble
- trust(s)/trusted
- turn us again
- ungodly
- upright
- vanity
- violence
- voice
- waters
- wicked
- wilderness
- will I
- within
- wondrous works
- word
- workers of iniquity
- works
- would
- wrath

The Psalms Organized by Category:

Hymn: 15, 24, 120, 121, 122, 123, 124, 125, 126, 127, 128, 129, 130, 131, 132, 133, 134.

Lament: 3, 4, 5, 6, 7, 9, 10, 12, 13, 14, 17, 22, 25, 26, 27, 28, 31, 35, 36, 38, 39, 41, 42, 43, 44, 51, 52, 53, 54, 55, 56, 57, 58, 59, 60, 61, 64, 69, 70, 71, 74, 77, 79, 80, 82, 83, 85, 86, 88, 90, 94, 102, 109, 137, 139, 140, 141, 142, 143.

Praise: 8, 29, 33, 46, 47, 48, 65, 66, 67, 68, 76, 81, 84, 87, 92, 93, 95, 96, 97, 98, 99, 100, 103, 104, 105, 106, 108, 111, 113, 114, 115, 117, 135, 136, 138, 145, 146, 147, 148, 149, 150.

Royal: 2, 18, 20, 21, 45, 72, 89, 101, 110, 144.

Thanksgiving: 30, 32, 34, 40, 75, 107, 116, 118.

Trust: 11, 16, 23, 62, 63, 91.

Wisdom: 1, 19, 37, 49, 50, 73, 78, 112, 119.

Bible study ideas:

1 Create a unique highlight to mark the contrasts between **godly** actions, attributes, ideas, or words and a different one to mark **ungodly** ones, *or* **good** versus **bad**.

2 Insert **your name** into the text whenever possible.

3 Draw a **triangle** over every reference to God, *e.g.* the Father, Son, Holy Spirit, Jesus, Christ, Holy One, King etc. and applicable pronouns *e.g.* he, him, his, I, you, your, yourself, etc.

4 Mark **repeated** words and phrases (see list).

Books of the Bible

#	Name	Abv	Chpt
1	Genesis	Ge	50
2	Exodus	Ex	40
3	Leviticus	Le	27
4	Numbers	Nu	36
5	Deuteronomy	De	34
6	Joshua	Js	24
7	Judges	Jg	21
8	Ruth	Ru	4
9	1 Samuel	1Sa	31
10	2 Samuel	2Sa	24
11	1 Kings	1Ki	22
12	2 Kings	2Ki	25
13	1 Chronicles	1Ch	29
14	2 Chronicles	2Ch	36
15	Ezra	Ez	10
16	Nehemiah	Ne	13
17	Esther	Es	10

Part 1 of 4

Blessed
is the man
that walks not
in the counsel
of the ungodly,
nor stands
in the way
of sinners,
nor sits
in the seat
of the scornful.

Psalm 1:1

How shall
a young man
cleanse his way?
by taking heed
according to
your word.
With my whole
heart have I
sought you:
O let me not
wander from your
commandments.
Your word have I
hid in my heart,
that I might not
sin against you.

Psalm 119:9-11

#	Name	Abv	Chpt
18	Job	Jb	42
19	Psalms	Ps	150
20	Proverbs	Pr	31
21	Ecclesiastes	Ec	12
22	Song of Solomon	So	8
23	Isaiah	Is	66
24	Jeremiah	Je	52
25	Lamentations	La	5
26	Ezekiel	Ez	48
27	Daniel	Da	12
28	Hosea	Ho	14
29	Joel	Jl	3
30	Amos	Am	9
31	Obadiah	Ob	1
32	Jonah	Jo	4
33	Micah	Mi	7
34	Nahum	Na	3

#	Name	Abv	Chpt
35	Habakkuk	Hb	3
36	Zephaniah	Zp	3
37	Haggai	Hg	2
38	Zechariah	Ze	14
39	Malachi	Ma	4
40	Matthew	Mt	28
41	Mark	Mk	16
42	Luke	Lk	24
43	John	Jn	21
44	Acts	Ac	28
45	Romans	Ro	16
46	1 Corinthians	1Co	16
47	2 Corinthians	2Co	13
48	Galatians	Ga	6
49	Ephesians	Ep	6
50	Philippians	Ph	4
51	Colossians	Cl	4

Part 3 of 4

Has this book made a difference? (Side 1 of 2)

We would LOVE to hear how this book has made a difference in your life. The personal experiences and testimonies of God working through His word encourages church/ministry volunteers as well as Chaplain Paula as she "ministers by mail," creating books to keep you "busy in the Bible."™

_____

_____

_____

_____

_____

_____

_____

_____

_____

_____

_____

_____

_____

_____

_____

_____

_____

_____

_____

_____

_____

_____

_____

_____

_____

_____

_____

_____

_____

What Biblically based workbook or features would you like to see offered?

_____

_____

Note: We share some letters and responses submitted to our ministry on "social media" to rally prayer and support for you and others but blot out identifying information (see exception below).

❏ Please pray for the prayer request included in this mailing.

❏ I will ask family/friends/media/social to support Renewing Lives.

❏ Please use 100% of my donation for the printing and mailing of your biblically based books to currently incarcerated persons.

With your signed permission (below) we might use what you write in one or more future printed publications or other forms of media or advertising.

OPTIONAL: As an adult, I grant permission to publish, in any form, all or part of my name with all or part of my comments (this page front & back) without compensation—allowing editing as needed.

X_____

Signature　　　　　Name Printed　　　　　Date

Mail to: Renewing Lives, PO Box **5529**, Diamond Bar, CA 91765-7529

Help us help others (page 1 of 2)

Please share how you found this book helpful, or how God used it to affect you:

_____

_____

_____

_____

_____

_____

_____

_____

_____

_____

_____

_____

_____

Is there anything you would add to this type of book to make it better?

_____

_____

In what ways, or for what purposes did you use this book:

_____

_____

Help us help others (page 2 of 2)

What Biblically based workbook or features would you like to see offered?

_____

_____

_____

Can you share a comment, complaint, idea, or suggestion?

_____

_____

Tell us if you noticed an error in need of correction:

_____

Note: We share some letters and responses submitted to our ministry on "social media" to rally prayer and support for you and others but blot out identifying information (see exception below.)

- ❏ Please pray for the prayer request included in this mailing.
- ❏ I will ask family/friends/media/social to support Renewing Lives.
- ❏ Please use 100% of my donation for the printing and mailing of your biblically based books to currently incarcerated persons.

With your signed permission (below) we might use what you write in one or more future printed publications or other forms of media or advertising.

OPTIONAL: As an adult, I grant permission to publish, in any form, all or part of my name with all or part of my comments (this page front & back) without compensation—allowing editing as needed.

✕ _____

Signature   Name Printed   Date

Mail to: Renewing Lives, PO Box **5529**, Diamond Bar, CA 91765-7529

Books of the Bible—Psalms

BOTB PsETRKJ LP20 061523

www.ingramcontent.com/pod-product-compliance
Lightning Source LLC
Chambersburg PA
CBHW081323090426
42737CB00017B/3019